The
Ghosts of the
Copper Queen Hotel

The
Ghosts of the
Copper Queen Hotel

A Journal of Actual Experiences from the Historic Copper Queen Hotel

A selection of eye-witness accounts written by the guests of this famous century-old hotel located in Bisbee, Arizona.

STARSYS PUBLISHING COMPANY

The Ghosts of the Copper Queen Hotel

WWW.GHOSTSOFTHECOPPERQUEEN.COM

Copyright © by Starsys Publishing Company - 2010
Front Cover Photo - Starsys
Interior Photos - Starsys
Historic Photos courtesy of the Copper Queen Hotel
Cover Design and Art Direction - Michael Nolan - *michaelnolanart.com*

The transcript of the following selected Ghost Journal entries was provided to Starsys Publishing Company by the management of the Copper Queen Hotel. The publisher performed an edit for grammatical structure, spelling and punctuation only, not content. The publisher makes no warrants or representations regarding the content of the materials provided herein.

Published by: Starsys Publishing Company
WWW.STARSYSPUBLISHING.COM
526 North Alvernon Way
Tucson, Arizona 85711

ISBN 10:   0982662246
ISBN 13:   9780982662243

Library of Congress Control Number: Pending

First Edition; August, 2010

Printed in the United States of America

Preface

It is with great pleasure that I am writing this preface to the following selection of stories from the Ghost Journals of the Copper Queen. The Copper Queen Hotel has always held a magical place in my heart. When my wife and I first visited this unique place many years ago, it was one of the most special and fondly-remembered weekends of our life together, and the hotel has become something very close to being our second home in the many years since that first experience.

We were initially captivated by the warmth, charm and grace of this century-old establishment, but immediately discovered, much to our delight, that we were not the only "loyal" guests of the Copper Queen. Yes … there are many repeat-guests who come from around the world to enjoy the beautiful rooms, wonderful food and old-west cachet of this historic treasure, but the guest register does not always contain the names of some of the others who walk these storied hallways.

For you see, the Copper Queen Hotel has captured not only the hearts and minds of some of its former guests, but some of their souls have decided to return, as well. One of our first experiences was a gentle one, and one that could easily be explained away as a coincidence. And yet, the way that it felt to us was something very different.

My wife and I are creatures of habit and absolutely love the routines that we develop. One of these was an evening ritual where we sat at our kitchen table, lit a large, white double-pillar candle which rested upon a glass base, and played cards together. This ritual became a nightly feature for us during many of our evenings. One day, we decided that a visit to Bisbee and to the Copper Queen might be a pleasant break. We reserved a room on the second floor, over the saloon and near the mezzanine (which is one of our favorite spots in the hotel).

We arrived early in the day and did some shopping on Main Street, followed by lunch. We then checked in and went up our room, noticing nothing unusual at that time. After my afternoon nap, we unpacked the deck of cards and decided to attempt to replicate our comfortable, card-playing routine in the mezzanine. Imagine our surprise when we left the room to find that there was a small, round table with two chairs, positioned in the alcove right outside our door … set up with a large, white double-pillar candle on a glass base! The candle was partially burned down to approximately (maybe exactly) the same point as was our candle at home.

We (of course) had not told any of the staff about our little ritual. We spent the evening playing cards at this table and, upon returning home, eventually moved on to some other evening pastimes. I should note that this arrangement with the candle was never replicated again and, in fact, on our next visit the table was no longer in the alcove.

Since that time many years ago, we have had increasingly spooky and intriguing experiences at the Copper Queen. The most powerful, beyond a doubt, took place in the Julia Lowell Room. Although the staff, by this time, knew of our fascination with the paranormal and supernatural, we had never asked to stay in this infamous room. One day, as we were checking out, the desk clerk inquired if we would like to take a look at the room so that we could decide if we would like to try it on our next visit.

I should point out that the room had already been documented on the television show - *Ghost Hunters* - and we had seen the rather famous video of the cast member's sheet being suddenly pulled off his leg as he slept in this room. We, naturally, said *yes* and excitedly went to the third floor. As we approached Room 315, neither of us felt anything out of the ordinary. But the instant that we turned the key and opened the door, both of us were battered with waves of emotion. Despite this, we entered the room. The feelings buffeting us could only be described as angry and upset.

Leaving quickly, we returned the key to the desk where we were told that over the years literally hundreds of people had stayed in this room and felt nothing unusual at all … while others reported benign, whimsical or even pleasant experiences with Julia. We have since thought that perhaps our experience might have been so powerful because I may coincidentally resemble the suitor from the past over whom Julia took her life.

In the following pages, you will find many selected stories from past guests, written in their own words. Some of them are innocuous … some are a bit unsettling … all of them will capture your imagination and convey the essence of a night at the Copper Queen Hotel.

John David Krygelski
Author of *The Harvest*
and *The Time Cursor*

List of Unregistered Guests

FIRST NAME: _____ Billy _____

LAST NAME: _____ Unknown _____

CHECK-IN DATE: _____ Unknown _____

CHECK-OUT DATE: _____ Open _____

STAFF COMMENTS:

Billy is believed to be a young boy of eight or nine It is said that he may have drowned in the San Pedro River and frequents the Copper Queen because his mother may have been a former employee, possibly in housekeeping or at the front desk.

GUEST COMPLAINTS:

It has been reported that he runs the hallways at all times of day or night, while laughing, and sometimes jiggles the doorknobs of guests' rooms.

There have been comments that he moves items in guests' rooms, sometimes just a little movement, sometimes from one table to the next; and that he likes to hide things in guests' rooms, such as a set of keys, later to replace them while the guests are out of the room.

Many guests claim that when they run bath water, they feel his presence and sometimes hear him cry.

He is never seen, just heard.

FIRST NAME: _____ Julia _____

LAST NAME: _____ Lowell _____

CHECK-IN DATE: _____ Unknown _____

CHECK-OUT DATE: _____ Open _____

STAFF COMMENTS:

Julia is, beyond a doubt, the most infamous of our guests. She appears to be in her early thirties. Julia was a "lady of the night," who plied her trade on Brewery Gulch, the raucous row of taverns adjacent to the Copper Queen, and frequently utilized some of our rooms as she "entertained" her customers. It is said that she became infatuated with one of her gentlemen, and when he did not return her affection, she took her own life at the Copper Queen. She has been actually seen by several of our guests.

GUEST COMPLAINTS:

Many guests have complained of smelling a cheap perfume in many areas of the hotel.

There have also been comments from some of the male guests that they have heard a whispering in their ear during their stay.

Both genders have reported her presence in their bed, and we have received many comments that she left her imprint in the bedding ... particularly at the foot of the bed.

We have also received reports that she has whisked off the covers from some men while they slept.

FIRST NAME: "Howard"

LAST NAME: Unknown

CHECK-IN DATE: Unknown

CHECK-OUT DATE: Open

STAFF COMMENTS:

We are not sure about the name *Howard*; it has only been felt by some as the name he prefers. He is older, tall and sports longer hair and a beard. He has often been observed on the fourth floor and is generally wearing a black over-cape and occasionally dons a top hat.

GUEST COMPLAINTS:

There are frequent reports of a strong, not unpleasant, cigar smell inside rooms and throughout the many common areas of the Copper Queen, especially the hallway on the fourth floor, adjacent to the Teddy Roosevelt Room.

A BRIEF HISTORY

Bisbee is the southernmost mile-high city in the United States. Old Town Bisbee is only two miles in length and less than one mile in width and is nestled in the picturesque Mule Mountains of Southern Arizona. Established in 1890, situated in a canyon surrounded by high desert mountains, Bisbee became known as one of the largest copper producing cities in the country, growing to over 20,000 residents by the 1920's, and was one of the largest cities between St. Louis and San Francisco.

The Phelps Dodge Mercantile opened their doors in the mid-1800's, supplying the locals and the mining industry with the various wares and food they needed. Not satisfied with being a small retail and food source for the town, the Phelps Dodge Mercantile started buying up some of the smaller mining expeditions in the area, to eventually become one of the largest mining camps in the world.

Hungry for further growth, Phelps Dodge, also known as the Copper Queen Mining Company, needed capital to finance its expansion and decided to build a hotel to lure investors to the area. Thus, the Copper Queen Hotel was conceived.

Construction of the Copper Queen Hotel was an arduous process in this rocky and mountainous terrain. She was started in 1898, and four years later opened her doors on George Washington's birthday, February 22, 1902. Built with an Italian motif, the hotel boasted seventy-two rooms with a bathroom at the end of each hallway. Eventually, each group of three rooms were remodeled so that the middle room, between the two others, could be converted into two private bathrooms, leaving the hotel with a total of forty-eight rooms. An elevator was added in the late-forties, necessitating the addition of a fifth floor to the hotel for the mechanical room. A swimming pool was constructed in the mid-seventies in the area that was used as a rear parking lot.

From its opening, the Copper Queen became the social and cultural centerpiece of the area. Parts of the hotel had many purposes, such as housing for the phone company operators and as a triage hospital for the historic Ft. Huachuca thirty miles away. The hotel has hosted Presidents and those hopeful to become President, along with many actors and actresses, and has been involved with the creation of much history and controversy in an area that for the longest of times had no laws to govern its citizens. Her doors have never once been locked throughout her long history, making the Copper Queen Hotel the longest continuously operating hotel in Arizona.

Date Unknown

> *When we walked into Room 315 (now the Julia Lowell Room), my son said immediately, "This is the ghost room." I got an overwhelming oppressive feeling and knew I didn't want to stay there. We changed rooms. It wasn't until the next day that we found out that indeed a ghost has been seen in that room, a woman dancing, who disappears when you try to touch her. Apparently, she only appears to single men, but I think she didn't like me "horning in" on her territory with my husband and my son, so she made me feel a bit uncomfortable. In hindsight, it would have been fun to see her, just not necessarily to spend the night with her!*
>
> *Cindy & Neal*

TABLE OF CONTENTS Page

December 31, 1999

~

December 31, 2000

Copper Queen Hotel
Ghost Journal

December 29ᵗʰ

    I climbed the back stairs while my husband was in the restroom. I walked by Room 207 and got the sense that it had known an evening with a "working girl" and a wild miner or cowboy (possibly with some shooting of a six-gun involved). When I got to the 4ᵗʰ floor, I walked to the front of the building and stood before a mirror. Up and to the left behind me I saw a smoky cloud. I do believe that it was a shadow of a past guest of the evening.

Virginia

January 2ⁿᵈ

Room 215, night of January 1ˢᵗ. The room filled with the smell of old rancid perfume. On two separate occasions the smell woke my wife, and footsteps were heard as if on a hard wood floor. On the morning of January 2ⁿᵈ while I was standing in front of the bathroom mirror, the shower curtain and rod flew off the wall and landed in the middle of the bathroom.

John & Helen

January 2ⁿᵈ

My husband and I took Room 315 and did not sleep well. Three or four times I was awakened by my husband's fears (moans & groans). He was really scared and said every time he fell asleep something or someone kept trying to take him away. Then he would yell for me. One time he started to speak and asked, "Who are you?" I replied, "I am a child of God," and started praying that we would make it through the night. We cut our visit short and left the next day.

M. Merino

January 2ⁿᵈ

We had a wonderful stay. No ghost stories this time, though. We will be back.

Mark & Cindy

January 3ʳᵈ

In Room 215 when we went to sleep, the shower curtain was closed totally. When we awoke the next morning, the shower curtain was open about a quarter of the way.

Robert

January 12ᵗʰ

Room 414 reported water on the bathroom floor and thought they saw a "shadow" of a little boy. They had the feeling he was crying. I think it might be the ghost of the boy who drowned in the San Pedro River.

Staff Member

January 28th

The fire alarm at the end of the hall went off at 11:30 p.m. I opened my door to check and heard voices. After five minutes, the alarm stopped. The couple in Room 304 left at midnight and didn't return. The front desk had no knowledge of any disturbances in the morning when we checked out.

Steve & Angela

February, 2nd

I woke up at 4:00 a.m. and saw Julia sitting on top of the enclosed TV cabinet, legs crossed, with her black dress lying beside her. She took a few sips from her bottle, smiled and left. She was breathing heavily and said, "You missed my dance."

Bob

February, 25th

On the night of February 25th in Room 315, I woke and smelled a distinct perfume odor. It wasn't until the morning that I found out the room I stayed in was the Julia Lowell room.

Joan

February, 28th

Room 302. After midnight for several minutes -- noises that sounded like things being pushed around and back and forth. Again on Tuesday, February 29th after midnight until about 3:00 a.m. – same sounds as if furniture was pushed along the floor back and forth. Then suddenly they quit.

Dolores

March, 4th

    Setting tables for morning breakfast. One light went off and on, and the door opened and then slammed shut. There were three bussers in the dining room.

Heather (Busser)

March, 18th

    My wife and I thoroughly enjoyed our trip. What a wonderful hotel. We did not have a ghostly experience but will try again next year.

Paul & Cheryl

March, 24th

    While staying in Room 306, I made sure the door was shut, locked, and deadbolted before I took my shower. When getting out of the shower, the door was ajar and the dead bolt off!!! I am detail-oriented and know the door was double-locked before my shower. My wife was asleep in the bed. I asked her about the door, and she was surprised as well, because she was asleep.

No Name

April, 5th

    My brother and I were sharing a room. I was petrified all night because of the ghost stories I had heard over dinner. About 11:00 p.m., an hour after we went to sleep, I heard a high-heeled footstep in the bathroom, immediately followed by something or someone rattling the bathroom supplies. I didn't get a wink of sleep that night.

Hilary

April, 5th

    At midnight the phone rang while we were sleeping. When we answered the phone, the only thing we heard was a noise and then nothing. Midnight is the bewitching hour, and if it was a ghost, he or she let us know they were watching over us. We really like our digs, Room 216, and know it is a special room.

No Name

April, 6ᵗʰ

     Room 209. At 4:00 a.m., the water started running in the bathroom. It ran for a couple of minutes, and when I got up, it stopped!!!

No Name

April, 10ᵗʰ

     Room 207, 1:00 a.m. I can't sleep. I begin to smell cheap perfume. Is it my after shave? It can't be! Still can't sleep, and it is hot. I begin to remove layers of blankets. Then something is pulling the first layer of covers under the bed. It's the ghost…it's here. I start a tug-o-war with the cover. I decide to let go. Shortly after, it starts again, the tug-o-war begins, and again I let go. The covers go under the bed. I just lay still for what seems like hours. I tell myself, "Be strong. It might not hurt you. Just be cool." The smell is back. I'm out of here. A quick shower and shave and so long. Did it take my covers because it knew I was hot?

Pete

April 11ᵗʰ

     While doing my job as a hostess and standing out front of the restaurant looking toward the staircase, I saw a little boy climb up and over the railing above and fall onto the stairs below. He was wearing a white t-shirt and blue shorts. He had dark hair and light skin. He looked to be about four years old. I ran over to check on him, but nothing was there.

Carey

April 15ᵗʰ

     What a great way to celebrate a birthday! No ghosts here tonight. At least I haven't seen any yet.

Jackie

April, 18th

  Room 406. We were trying to fall asleep, my best friend and I, in the same bed. It had been close to two hours since we had attempted to get some shuteye. There were two distinguishing noises. First, this boy was crying repeatedly. It could not have been done by a real boy because it lasted so long and ended with a soft whistle afterwards. Secondly, there were three huge, loud booms consecutively, sounding like a big dresser or desk falling over three times. It seemed like it was right near our door on the 4th floor. We didn't get to sleep until 3:00 a.m. The fact that we both heard these noises, not just one of us, makes it all more real.

Janelle & Nachelle

April 23rd

  Room 402 (top floor). Heard footsteps over our heads around 2:30 a.m.

No Name

April 23rd

  Room 301. Heard footsteps and jumping noises over our heads around 2:30 a.m.

Lisa

April 25th

  Room 302. Beginning at 5:00 a.m. and lasting about twenty minutes, we heard dull thuds and banging in the corner near the table-/desk. Sounded like it came from the corner or in the wall! Sounded like someone opening and closing a desk drawer.

Don

April 25th

  While braiding my hair, I noticed one of my rubber bands missing. I searched for it and found it way under the nightstand. How did it get that far under the nightstand?

Krystal

May 10th

     Room 407. At 11:30 p.m. above the TV sat a foggy figure. I did not want to believe, so I went back to sleep. About 2:30 a.m. I awoke again to see the same figure. I went back to sleep to awake in the morning to see what the picture was above the TV. There was none.

Brad

May 12th

     We left our room at 8:30 p.m. or so. We left about five pairs of shoes by the door in a pile. We returned at 2:00 a.m. to find them in a neat line by the door. HOW DID THAT HAPPEN?

Sherri

May 21st

     At 2:45 a.m. I turned our fan on high. Within one minute it turned itself off and on again. It happened a second time about two minutes later. No electric problems reported from the hotel.

No Name

May 30th

     Last night I locked the deadbolt on the inside of our room; however, I didn't put the chain lock on. Later I found the chain locked.

Susan

May 31st

     Last night there were lots of bumps, slamming of doors, and a vacuum went on and off at about 2:00 a.m. When we went to our room earlier, the ghost had visited us. We could smell her perfume, and the clock was messed up. We were the only ones in that wing, and it sounded like people were all around us.

No Name

June 3rd

     I smelled perfume in my room when we first checked in. Our

room door was ajar when we first got to the room. I smelled the same perfume by the elevator door on the 3rd floor. Felt tingling in my scalp and other parts of my body. The hair on my arms and legs stood straight up.

Mike

June 5th

Great hotel, great experience. Can't wait to come back.

Chuck

June 14th

Who was the lady dressed in black with long, black hair seen floating silently on the mezzanine toward Room 211 at 3:00 a.m?

No Name

June 14th

Room 211. The clock was set back at certain times during the night. At one point the clock read 2:00 a.m. I was feeding my baby and noticed the time. What I thought to be two hours later, I again got up to feed my baby. The clock still read 2:00 a.m. However, when we awoke in the morning, the clock had the same time as my watch.

Taylor

June 15th

Around 3:30 a.m. there was a soft tap on the door but it seemed very gentle. I felt unafraid, yet still I did not get up to answer it. The windows at one time moved up and down very slightly.

A Guest

June 26th

The alarm clock went off in the middle of the night for no reason. We hadn't set it, and it was even in the *off* mode.

Tatiana

June 30th

The glass holding the toothpicks in the dining room all of a sudden fell off the stand. It is usually placed on the right side of the stand, but it had fallen off of the left side.

R.N.

July 8th

We stayed in the Julia Lowell Room 315. My husband came into the room, and I told him we were in the "Ghost Room." He said, "Oh, I don't know about that stuff." At that moment, the window shade flew open. "I do believe in ghosts…I do believe in ghosts….I do, I do, I do believe in ghosts."

Laura

July 10th

Room 412. We checked in late, ate dinner and watched a little TV, then went to bed. The phone rang twice, and there was no one on the other end. Just as the second call came in, the fire alarm went off. The front desk said the alarms had not gone off anywhere in the building.

No Name

July 15th

    My husband John and I stayed in Room 413 on 12-11-99. I woke up in the middle of the night and went to open the window. I heard three loud, rhythmic knocks on the wall behind me... John was sleeping soundly. I didn't think too much of it at the time, but our friends in the next room informed me the next morning that they also heard the knocks coming from our room. This trip we had no experiences to share.

Lorraine & John

July, 22nd

    If you listen, you can hear them talking.

Reanna

July, 30th

    Room 304. Wonderful room and hotel. Much activity of spirits walking through the door -- all men dressed in period attire of early twenties, formal and WWI attire. Too many to count. Looked like they were here to view a body in the room. Coins fell from the ashtray, and a cup fell over.

Phil

August 5th

    First day upon arrival, I set my alarm. It never went off until the third day I was here. Why? I never touched it!

Jill

August 5th

    Stayed in Room 213. We never touched the closet door, yet it was opened when we woke up in the morning. The door has to have quite a bit of pressure to open!!!

Linda & Mary

August 7th

Great stay. Can't wait to come back.

Jack

August 9th

Room 409. Nothing happened in our room during our stay, yet it felt like someone was watching us the whole time. It sent chills down our backs. It was a great stay, though! Bisbee is beautiful.

Steph, Gary and the Kids

August 10th

Even though we did not tell our kids about the ghost sightings here at the hotel, at dinner tonight our three-year-old went on and on about the "little boy" who held his hand as we walked around the building this evening. He said the little boy told him "he had fallen in the hotel."

Tom, Joy and Kids

August 11th

Room 210. My sister and I were sleeping in one bed, and my dad was in the other. Around 2:00 a.m., my dad woke with goose bumps all over. He said that his hair was standing on end. When he tried to go back to sleep, the goose bumps continued. When he ignored those, he claimed he felt pressure on his back like someone was trying to wake him up.

No Name

August 17th

Room 202. We went out to dinner and left the window open. (I know I left the window open.) When we returned about two hours later, the window was closed. The next morning (August 18th) my girlfriend was taking a shower and her purse was on the bed, zipped up. I had already left. When she got out of the shower, her credit card was laying on the floor. She swears she didn't take it out of her purse, and I know beyond any shadow of doubt I didn't close the window and neither did any hotel staff. I checked.

Michael

August 18th

　　Room 401. Around 2:00 a.m. a female voice said something on the left side of my bed. My daughter-in-law was sound asleep to the right of me. "Pretty scary."

Janice

August 18th

　　We were staying in Room 315, and at 2:34 a.m. I was awakened with a start. I felt a long, curly beard on my face. For a few seconds I could not move. Then I sat straight up in bed and could see a very tall, dark image looking at me. By 2:36 a.m. the event was over.

Annie

August 23rd

　　Set TV to sleep at ninety minutes. TV shut off after thirty minutes. I just ignored it and went to sleep. Two hours later I awoke to the TV on and showing thirty minutes to shut-off time. STRANGE!!!

No Name

August 24th

　　I didn't hear anything strange in my room, but the times on the clock kept changing and the volume on the TV would go up and down.

No Name

August 25th

Great place, but the clocks were different times all over the place.

Duke

August 30th

At 5:30 p.m. my mom sent me down to collect some extra pillows and towels for our stay. I took the stairs down to the desk. Upon reaching the 3rd floor, I got the feeling I was being followed. On my way back up I took the elevator, I pressed *4* and a few seconds later I ended up on the 3rd floor. As the door opened I saw that nobody was there. Then I heard footsteps and a woman's laughter. I think Julia was having some fun.

Fabien

September 2nd

My husband and I started out in Room 212 and decided to switch to a different room, Room 305. While I was occupied doing something, my husband was in the room about to turn on the TV, and all of a sudden it came on all by itself. Totally weird, but exciting. After all, what did I come here for?

Mindy

September 5th

We stayed in Room 212 last night and experienced some strange happenings with the hall's overhead light. While we were watching TV, the light was shining into our room from the window over the door. My husband said he wanted that light to go out because it was shining in his eyes. A minute later at 8:35 p.m. the light went out. For the next two hours the light would go on and then off. While this was happening, no other lights were affected. The last time it came on, it stayed on until we went to bed. This morning there was no unusual activity with that light at all.

Val & Jim

September 6th

    Room 210. Very quiet until 2:00 in the morning when the light on the table came on by itself. My roommate blamed it on a loose light bulb. But you and I know the truth!!!

Mike and Keith

September 22nd

    My husband and I came to Bisbee and did not have reservations at the Copper Queen. The young lady working the front desk said we were in luck because Room 213 was available. She gave us the key so we could view it before agreeing to take it. After check-in, we went to look at the pool on the 2nd floor and so that my husband could have a smoke. We left the door wide open. It was opened so far it was braced by a pipe. (In other words, you would have to either pull on it or give it a good push to close it.) It was 3:30 in the afternoon. There was no wind and no breeze. We were by the steps that lead down to the pool, and as we looked at the pool, the door slammed shut. I ran to the door, and no one was there. We went back later to further inspect the door and found no springs, wires or loose hinges. We propped the door open again and turned our backs on it. I turned around quickly and saw the door was slamming shut. Not only was no one there, but also the speed in which it was closing actually slowed down as I stood there watching it. The next morning we woke up and decided to take pictures on the 2nd floor mezzanine. Two large windows were open (both the same width), and I thought a picture of me sitting on the windowsill would be nice. I walked up the stairs to approach the windowsill, and to my surprise, the window slammed shut in my face! The scary thing is that the other window remained open. If the wind had blown the window shut, why didn't the other one move?

Marie & Tom

October 9th

    Room 302. We had to switch rooms at 4:00 a.m. after we saw a tall woman in antique clothing standing in the bathroom door.

Cheryl

October 11ᵗʰ

     Room 413. We woke up to find our door unlocked and opened in the morning. My husband swears that the door was closed and locked prior to going to bed. The housekeeping staff had not started to work at the time we woke up.

Sarah

October 15ᵗʰ

     Room 314. Around 4:00 a.m. there was knocking at my dad's door to his room. He said he kept asking who was there, but there was no answer. Finally, he opened the door and still no one was there.

Susan

October 21ˢᵗ

     Room 315. After arriving at the hotel, we settled into our room and then went out site seeing. When we came back to our room later that evening, we were greeted with the scent of wax candles that had just been blown our. The thing is that we didn't have any candles in our room.

Mark

October 27ᵗʰ

     Room 315. On our way out of our room, I saw what I thought might be Julia (the ghost) out of the corner of my eye. I whirled around and watched as she faded into the wall.

Fred & Betty

November 4ᵗʰ

     Room 213. While using our Ouija board, we came into contact with three entities. The first had slow movements of the Ouija board and gave us limited information. The second spirit identified herself as a presence on the 1st floor. She claimed to have been born in 1940 and died in 1969. Her movements along the board were much smoother than the first. She enjoyed turning the pancetta in several directions. The third being appeared as a childlike energy that gave us its name as "Hillary." The child swung the pancetta around the board similar to a delighted child on a swing. The birth date for this being was in 1923, and it left the room before answering the year of her death. After we spoke with these three, the first appeared once more. We began asking questions but simply received the answer, "Just leave me be." We were ok with that. The energy of this presence was that of an older man. The picture in both of our heads was an old miner, scruffy beard and all. We put down the board and proceeded to venture out into the building to possibly sneak a peek of one of the spirits we had just been in contact with. Later in the evening, something or someone pounded on our bedroom wall. It wasn't until the next morning at check-out that we found out there are supposed to be three ghosts here at the hotel.

Kiera & Jeremiah

November 7th

Room 315. My husband and I could hear someone walking around our room, and then the door opened and closed all by itself.

Sherry & John

November 11th

We could not unlock our room door, seemed that the dead bolt was locked from the inside. We could hear noise coming from our room. My husband went to the front desk as I stayed and watched the door to see who might come out. When my husband returned with the front desk clerk and she tried to open the door, it opened right up, and no one was in the room.

Lisa

December 12th

Room 210. The night started out just fine until about 11:00 p.m. when the lights started to flicker as we were watching TV. Of course it was blamed on a loose light bulb, but my sister checked and it was in good and tight. Then I was awakened at 2:37 a.m., feeling a pushing on my head, kind of like someone was trying to wake me up, but there wasn't anyone there. The room was a little creepy, but I had a wonderful time.

Lauren

December 15th

Stopped in just on a whim, what a wonderful stay.

Jose

December 18th

Room 305, 2:45 a.m. We could not sleep, so we decided to take a walk around the hotel. We left our room and locked the door. When we returned to our room, the door was unlocked and ajar. Nothing was missing, but my makeup was moved from the bathroom to the bed. Needless to say, we did not get any sleep this night.

Lisa

December 27th

Room 303. First time my husband and I stayed at the Copper Queen. Last night there was a strong smell of a cigar. Later in the night my husband smelled a strong perfume, which I could not smell myself. I have complete hair loss and have to wear a wig, which is short in length. This morning when I woke up, I found a bobby pin on my pillow. I have no use for them. Where did it come from? Or who put it there?

Brenda

January 1, 2001
~
December 31, 2001

Copper Queen Hotel

Ghost Journal

January 3rd

My brother-in-law and I were staying in Room 210. At about 12:30 a.m. while we were watching TV, the bedside lamp started to flicker. About two minutes later the light went out. We thought the light bulb had just burned out, but my brother-in-law noticed that the switch was now in the *off* position, and was able to turn it back on with the switch. How could it have gotten turned off?

Seth

January 9th

My husband and I have stayed at the Copper Queen many times with no ghostly encounters. However, on this trip in Room 411 we were both awakened at 3:00 a.m. to the feeling of someone trying to get into bed with us. Just as we turned the light on, we both smelled perfume and a very faint sound of a woman singing. All of this was within a five-minute time frame.

Abby & Mark

January 18th

Room 406. My wife was in the bathroom, taking a late night shower at about midnight. I was reading when I saw the silhouette of a man come out of the bathroom and disappear in front of the room's main door.

Carl

February 1st

Room 214. At 3:00 a.m. my wife and I were awakened with a jolt to find our room freezing cold and the chair moved across the room and in front of the door. The heater was working just fine and showed 72 degrees on the thermostat. As soon as I moved the chair back to where it belonged, the room started to warm up again.

Brian

February 14th

A real jewel Bisbee and the Copper Queen Hotel are. From the moment we checked into our Room 316, I felt a spirit. I awakened at 12 midnight and then again at 3:00 a.m. This time I saw a shadow go across the room. There is definitely a presence in this room, and a nice one at that.

Madeline

February 16ᵗʰ

Room 315. Oh, my! Unbelievable! We checked in at 4:00 p.m. and noticed a stale, old-smelling perfume in the room. We left and wandered the town and went to dinner. We returned to our room at about 10:00 p.m. to find our CD player on and playing music. My mother took her ring off before going to bed. When we woke up, her ring was on MY finger!!! No joke. We will be back. We had a great time and enjoyed it all.

Karen & Dorothy

February 19ᵗʰ

I witnessed a person and felt that he was behind me as I walked down the main staircase of the hotel. When I turned around to say *hi*, there was no one there.

Fre

February 21ˢᵗ

I was waiting for someone to bring more cream for the complimentary coffee when a figure of a young man breezed past me and said, "Good Morning."

Stella

March 8ᵗʰ

I have a weird feeling about this place.

Holly

March 27ᵗʰ

While I was in the bathroom brushing my teeth, I heard the door open and then close behind me. I was staying by myself, so I turned, expecting to see maid service in my room. The room was empty and there was no one in the hallway.

Mark

April 9th

     Room 414. At about 10:30 p.m. we smelled a very strong cigar smell. The next morning when we opened the door to leave for the day, something ran or floated past us very fast into the room, fast enough to make a whooshing sound. We checked the room and found nothing, so we left. When we returned the windows were open, we know we closed them before we left for the day.

Marline

April 10th

     This letter arrived from a former guest along with a photograph: We stayed at your beautiful hotel for one night on March 19, 2001, where we enjoyed Bisbee and the elegant dinner and luxurious breakfast very much. After a long drive to get there, we were very tired and fell into a deep sleep the moment we hit the pillows. Very early a mysterious draft and a strange feeling among the blankets awakened me. Since it was an exceptionally bright and sunny morning, we decided to get up and enjoy the sights of your sleepy little town. My husband took a photo of our old-fashioned room with me still in bed and must have disturbed a spirit that was still in our room. In this photo (now missing) it looks as if a body is just passing through the wall.

Rosita & Rudolf
Guests from Germany

April 25th

     I was awakened with a start. I thought I heard water running. I sat up in bed and heard a small child crying and calling, "Mommy, Mommy," only twice and then it stopped.

No Name

May 18th

     My fiancé and I were sleeping and were awakened at 2:30 a.m. I felt a presence in the room but could not explain my feelings to my fiancé. The room was hot, so we turned on the air conditioning to high, but it kept turning off. Still hot, we fell in and out of sleep. Finally, at 3:30 in the morning , frustrated from no sleep, I turned on the light to get up for the day. When the light went on, I noticed that one of the charms from my necklace was on the floor across the room. The charm has a Buddha on one side and in Japanese characters on the back it reads, "May you be safe wherever you go." It has not left my necklace since I got it in San Francisco eight years ago. Not only that, but the loop where the charm goes through looked as if it had been pulled apart.

Leslie

May 18th

Room 402. Walking down the hallway on my way back to my room with coffee, someone tapped me on the shoulder. Startled, I dropped the coffee and turned to see who was there. No one was in the hall.

Marsha

May 24th

We were fast asleep when we were awakened by a noise. Somehow the jewelry I had on the desk was picked up and then dropped onto the floor.

Patty & Gary

May 27th

Room 402, 2:00 a.m. On my way down to the front desk to get an extra pillow, there was a little boy walking down the hallway in front of me. I called out to him to see if he was lost. No answer. He went around the corner ahead of me by about five feet. When I turned the corner, he was gone.

Cory

June 6th

Room 310. Had a very interesting visit. The TV was not on, and you could still hear voices and music coming from it. Second, my cell phone disappeared, and all my socks plus a pair of warm-up pants. This morning the socks were found in Room 306 (a vacant room). We were staying in Room 310. We never found the rest of my things.

Jude

June 7th

My friend and I were sitting at the bar, having a drink and talking with the bartender. We were the only ones there. Suddenly, it sounded like a lot of people were in the room, and we saw a flash of light. Then it was quiet again.

Jim

June 10th

Room 402. While reading in my room at about 11:30 p.m., I heard what sounded like a drawer opening in the bathroom. When I went in to check, one of the drawers was open. I gave it no thought and went to bed. When I awoke in the morning, all the drawers were open.

Wendy

June 13th

Pick Room 217. He's friendly!

No Name

June 28th

Room 312. At 3:00 a.m. I was awakened by my husband pushing me on my back, almost like he was trying to push me out of bed. I turned over to ask what he was doing, and he was fast asleep in the room's other bed. In the morning he told me he moved because he thought I was pushing on him.

Chelsea & Jim

June 28th

While doing my nightly walk of the building at 8:30 p.m. the door handle to Room 304 jiggled. You could see that someone was trying to pull the door open. This room does not have a guest staying in it.

Front Desk Clerk - No Name

June 29th

I wanted to check out the pool area and take a swim. I went to the door that said *EXIT* over it. On the way down that hall I felt a chill, almost felt like someone was there. I went up the stairs and was just about to open the doors to go out, and the door flew open, and then shut. I decided not to go swimming this trip.

No Name

July 12th

Room 312. This was our second trip here to the hotel. We were sitting in our room; my wife was watching the television, and I was reading a magazine. My Gatorade bottle that was half-full slid across our table and stopped right on the edge of the table.

Taylor

July 12th

Room 312. I was trying to fall asleep. It was 1:00 a.m. I heard moaning sounds, almost like a crying noise, coming from the left corner of our room. The moaning was definitely coming from our room and not the room next door.

Sue

July 15th

Room 412. I woke up at 2:30 a.m. to the sound of a little child laughing. As soon as I turned on the light and sat up in bed, the laughing stopped. I sat up for a while and did some reading. When I decided to go back to bed and turned off the light, I heard the window latch open, and the laughing started again and kept going for about a minute or two.

No Name

July 21st

Room 312. The first night of our stay just as we were getting ready for bed, we heard what sounded like some one playing with marbles. My husband was awakened with a start; he said it felt like someone was tapping him on the shoulder. Our second night we heard the marbles again and could not sleep.

No Name

August 19th
        Some time between 2:00 a.m. and 10:00 a.m. my bag of corn chips found itself strewn about the floor! The armchair we had in our room was moved up close to the door.

Steven

August 28th
        After a long and exhausting day of site seeing and traveling, I finally went to bed. At about 3:30 a.m. I felt something nudge me, causing me to wake up. I felt some sort of presence on the side of the bed as though someone sat down. I turned over and saw an outline of something or someone. It started to become clearer, and I became aware of coat lapels and a hat. It looked like a gentleman. I heard the doorknob move and looked over to find an outline of a woman standing there. I looked back toward the gentleman and he was gone, looked back toward the door and she was gone.

No Name

September 15th
        Room 311, 12:30 a.m. The adjoining door lock rattled, then the door slowly opened, and then closed. I spent the rest of the night with a friend in another room. Maintenance checked the door the next morning and informed us that the door is deadbolted from the inside out, and no one was staying in the adjoining room.

No Name

October 1st
        Room 305. When we left our room to go downstairs for dinner,

we made sure our door was locked and secure. When we got back to our room, the door was ajar.

No Name

October 18th

Room 315. My husband and I checked in earlier today, we had a lovely evening in town and returned to our room and went to bed. At some point in the night I awoke to find my husband at the door to our room. "What's the matter?" I asked. "I saw a woman walk from the window and through the door," he said. "Don't be silly," I said. I looked at the clock; it was 2:05 a.m. We turned the light on, and the door was still locked. Just then I heard a woman laugh from  the hallway. We opened the door just in time to see the hem of a black skirt disappear up the staircase. We ran up to see who the woman was, but she was gone!

Linda & Bill

October 30th

Our first time here and loved it! Today is my birthday, and I thought I had lost a pair of sapphire earrings in the sink. We looked and had maintenance look also. We could not find them, and I thought they were gone for good. Later my husband had to stand on top of the toilet to get a box of tissue off the top shelf, and there were my earrings.

Debbie & Bob

November 12th

My friend and I were awakened at 2:30 a.m. by an urgent knock at the door. When I responded, a woman asked for Dorothy. When I said she had the wrong room, we heard nothing else. She knocked on no other doors, and we did not hear her walk away. We opened the door, and there was no one in the hall.

Teddy

November 21ˢᵗ
Fantastic stay, can't wait to come back

Paul & Cindy

December 15ᵗʰ
Room 210. I awoke around 2:45 a.m. due to my brother's snoring. I was just about to wake him up when I looked up toward the ceiling and saw a faint blue ball of light descending toward me. It caught me by surprise; I just stared at it for a while. When I tried to move or talk, it pressed itself against me. I tried yelling, but nothing would come out. Every hair on my body was on end, I had goose bumps, and I was so cold. None of us could get back to sleep last night. We kept hearing noises.

David

December 23ʳᵈ
Immediately after retiring, I heard two long scratches, which caused me to sit up and look around. I noticed small flashing lights on the ceiling and woke my husband to behold the phenomenon. He said, "Congratulations, dear, you've located the smoke alarm."

Martha & Alan

January 1, 2002

~

December 31, 2002

Copper Queen Hotel
Ghost Journal

January 15th

    While wandering around on the second floor, I felt someone hit me in the shoulder, yet no one was around. Immediately I was stricken with an intense headache. I quickly went downstairs, and as soon as I was out of the building the headache went away.

Dana

January 30th

    Room 315. My experiences had no visual sightings of apparitions. When I arrived and put my shoes under the bed, it felt like I had put my hand in water. I pulled my hand out and it was dry. When I pushed my items under the bed again, I received the same sensation. I placed some sage branches in a V-shape on the dresser top. When I looked again, one leg of the V was moved about three inches away from the V formation. I checked and this was but a result of air circulation. Not able to sleep I sat and read for a while. Around 3:30 a.m. I heard noise in the hall and went out to look. I witnessed a green and soft blue light formation on the wall by the exit sign. As soon as I saw it, it was gone.

No Name

January 31st

    We checked in at evening time and enjoyed eating in the restaurant. My friend and I decided to shower at night to save some time in the morning. While she was in the shower, I tried to put the TV on, but nothing -- the remote wouldn't work. I checked the plug and even tried the power switch on the actual TV, but it just would not go on. I just sat quietly and suddenly was filled and over come by a warmth, actually lots of heat, just as suddenly the TV came on. The spirits enjoy "living" here.

Patty

February 11th
Room 406. We did not see any physical evidence of a ghost; however, the blind in our room went up and down twice on its own, very, very slowly.

Sarah

February 17th
Room 401, 2:45 a.m. As my husband and I were relaxing and watching some TV, we heard a very faint tapping. It sounded like it came from the bathroom. Then the two of us noticed the door handle to our room door turning and the door start to open. My husband called out and said, "Someone is in this room. You must have the wrong one." The door continued to open. My husband jumped up, went to the door and pulled it the rest of the way open. No one was there or in the hallway. Before my husband got the door closed, we heard the laughter of what sounded like a couple of little kids in the hallway.

Kathy

February 22nd
Room 412. After I took a shower, an outline of a face appeared very clearly on the heavily steamed-up mirror. I could not tell if it was a man or a woman. Later that evening we heard a moaning noise coming from the bathroom. After turning on the light, the noise stopped; however, the light would not turn off even with the switch turned off. Shortly after midnight the moaning began again. This morning we were able to turn the light off.

Marsha

February 24ᵗʰ

　　We loved the hotel. While I was not bothered by the "ghost," my husband was. Things ended up missing this morning -- first, the mine-tour tickets he had in his wallet, then his key to the room and a small trinket he carried with him. We decided to go to breakfast and hopefully remember where he put these things. Upon getting back to our room, all of the missing objects were sitting right on the top of the desk.

Sharon

February 24ᵗʰ

　　Main dining room. We arrived late for lunch (just before the restaurant closed), but the waiter let us in even after they closed the doors. While eating, we noticed the doors open and close two different times with no one there.

Kathy

March 11th

Room 401. While watching TV late at night around 2:00 a.m., the volume would go up and then down. When I would get up to check it, I actually had to turn the sound up or down myself, so this showed me it was not an internal problem with the set it self. After about an hour of this, I turned off the TV and went to bed. At 4:00 a.m. I was awakened by the TV turning itself on.

Joe

March 12th

Room 315. At different times my wife and I both felt a tugging on our left feet.

No Name

March 23rd

Room 207. At 2:00 a.m. I heard a saxophone playing a very sad but beautiful song and I could hear a woman weeping. I got up and put on my robe and looked around the room. No one was there! I decided to check the hall. I opened my door and walked into the hallway. I walked up and down and out into the foyer -- nothing but the song.

Terry

March 23rd

Prayer of Jabez:
Oh lord, bless me indeed and enlarge my territory. Place your hand on me and you would keep me from evil, that I may not cause pain.

No Name

March 26th

Room 305. The phone rang at exactly 12 midnight. My husband woke to answer it, and all he heard was a series of beeps. We had turned on the light at this time, so I went to the bathroom. The phone was silent the whole time I was there. When we turned off the lights, no sooner did we get settled than the phone rang again!! The time now was 12:05 a.m. We turned on the light and answered it -- same weird beeps. This time my husband went into the bathroom. The phone never rang again afterwards. We called the front desk, and they said they had no explanation, just that sometimes at random the phones ring at exactly midnight.

Maryann

April 16ᵗʰ

You hear things moving and creaking in the night.

Amanda

April 16ᵗʰ

Room 211. I was awakened at 2:00 a.m. by some kind of sound, along with a very faint smell of perfume. I noticed a white fog in the far corner of the room. I tried to move and talk to my girlfriend but could not move whatsoever. After about thirty seconds, the fog just drifted off. However, the smell of the perfume lingered until dawn.

Chris

April 21ˢᵗ

A glass of wine, placed squarely in front of us on a table in the saloon, moved at least two to three inches with all of us watching it and no one touching it. This was before we even sipped our first drink!!!

Lana

May 3ʳᵈ

Relaxing before going to bed for the night, we were watching the TV. It was just about 9:00 p.m., and the TV turned itself off. The remote was two feet away

.

No Name

May 27ᵗʰ

Room 303. Well now, I must say that we did not see a spirit, but last night at 3:03 a.m. I heard water, like someone was running water or taking a shower in the next room. Who takes showers at 3:03 a.m.? Anyway, I got up to use the bathroom, and on my way out I noticed a bit of steam on the mirror. I felt down to the hot side faucet of the sink and it was HOT, as if someone had the faucet on for a while. Now explain that.

No Name

June 19th

    At 3:00 a.m. I was awakened by a very, very cold draft, like a breeze coming through the room. (The windows were closed, and it is June.) I could not go back to sleep the rest of the night. It felt like I was being watched. In the morning my room key, that I had placed on the desk, was missing.

Dillon

June 21st

    After a very long day on the road, I thought I would get a good night's sleep. I woke up at 2:00 a.m. I thought I heard someone call my name. I dozed off again for just a few minutes and heard it again. At this point I could not fall asleep again, so I decided to go up to the 3rd floor balcony and relax. As I sat for a while, I started to doze off once again, only to hear this woman's voice one more time. When I looked up, across the street atop of the building next to the large staircase was a white, transparent mist that had the form of a lady dressed in some sort of white uniform. As I stood to get a better look, it disappeared into the night. In the morning I found out this building was the nursing quarters for the hospital in days past.

Michael

June 30th

    Room 301. We went to bed rather early, at approximately 10:00 p.m. At 12 midnight we heard a very loud noise, like a door slamming. Suddenly, the bed side lamp went on and the air conditioner turned off. The bathroom door was closed. (We had left it open.) I got up to see what had happened and found that somehow the switch on the lamp had actually been turned to the *on* position, and the air conditioner switch had been turned to *heat*. HOW?

Sean

July 4th

What a great hotel. We came for one day and decided to stay three.

Tim & Sue

July 6th

Room 402, 4:00 a.m. A child's voice calling "Mom" broke my sleep. Ten minutes later something or someone tugged the blanket on the bed.

Carla

July 6th

Room 401. Around 1:30 a.m. I heard something outside my room. It sounded like spurs or two pieces of metal rubbing against one another. I went and looked through the peephole, but nothing was there. When I turned around, I saw a figure in the mirror, with black hair. Around 3:00 a.m. I felt something move (like sitting down) on my bed.

Stephanie

July 12th

Unable to sleep, I took a walk around the hotel around 3:00 a.m. On the third floor landing, I stopped and looked in the mirror. Not only did I see my reflection, there was that of an older gentleman to the side. Startled, I turned around only to find no one there.

J.J.

July 17th

    Room 212. Our TV shut off twice last night for no reason. This morning our smoke alarm went off for no reason???

Jennifer and David

July 17th

    While exploring the hotel, I suddenly felt a presence, as if I was being followed. When I turned around, all I saw was a shadow on the wall. I turned back around and ran like the dickens and vowed never to revisit the shadow on the 3rd floor again.

No Name

July 17th

    Room 313, our first night of a three-night stay. After we were in bed with the lights out, the ceiling fan light came on. We actually had to get up and turn it off.

John and Phyllis

July 21st

    My husband and I were sitting on the 3rd floor balcony when we heard the window from Room 311 open and close several times. When we looked into the room, there was no one there!!!

Dorothy and Kevin

August 4th

    I woke up a little after 2:00 a.m. when the air conditioner came on all of a sudden. (I had not turned it on since I checked in.) I went to the bathroom, and the right-hand cabinet door under the sink was wide open. Neither my wife nor I had touched it, and it was not open when we went to bed around midnight.

Jason

August 15ᵗʰ

Room 406. I went to bed around 11:30 p.m. After a while nature called, and I got up to go to the bathroom. Everyone else was still asleep in the room. Returning to bed and lying down, I rolled to my left side and saw a tall man or woman standing next to the window looking at me. There was no facial features, just an outline that was whitish and transparent. I was able to awaken my friend, yet he could not see anything. As I was still lying there about an hour later, the form appeared again, until I heard three light taps on the wall. Then it was gone.

Steven

August 25ᵗʰ

Room 318. What a great place! Didn't see any ghosts, but heard a lot of footsteps and noises that started around 3:00 a.m, until about 5:00 a.m.

Steve

September 2ⁿᵈ

Room 301. At approximately 9:45p.m. the fire alarm went off intermittently for no reason. We all walked out of the room and saw that no one else's alarm was going off. When we went back into our room, it stopped going off.

Jan

September 7ᵗʰ

Last night around 8:30 p.m. I went up to the 3rd and 4th floors and took photos of the hallways, etc. When I got back to our room, my husband was laying on the bed, watching TV. I reached up to turn the fan down, and the light globe fell onto my husband's leg, cutting him on the ankle. He had a deep L-shaped cut on his ankle and smaller cuts on both legs, along with a bruised ankle. His injuries were much worse than they should have been. After checking the light fixture, all the screws that held the globe in place were there and screwed all the way in. The globe should not have fallen by itself!!!

Stella

September 27ᵗʰ

Room 315. Our room smelled of a sweet lilac most of the night. My daughter felt something tug on her sleeve around midnight. I was awakened by a cool breeze at 3:00 a.m. and watched as our closet door opened on its own. You could see the hangers move a bit, and then the door closed very, very slowly.

No Name

October 9ᵗʰ

Thank God I didn't see or hear anything!!!

Marietta

October 13ᵗʰ

I was taking a shower and noticed the water kept getting hotter. I thought maybe it was just the shower, but it just kept getting hotter and hotter. Just to see, I turned the water all the way to cold and turned to rinse the shampoo out of my hair. About ten seconds later the water started to get very hot again. I turned around, and the shower knob was turned all the way to the hot side, and the shower curtain was opened about six inches. When I got out of the shower, I felt like I was being watched and then noticed an image of a woman in the bathroom mirror, but when I turned to look again, she was gone.

Laurie

October 14ᵗʰ

Room 315. Our first night here at the hotel, it seemed like my husband had a very restless night sleep (or so I thought). He kept moving all over the bed. In the morning he thanked me for giving him "such nice fondling through out the night." I thought he was joking when he said this, and he thought I was pulling his leg when I told him I had done no such thing. On our second night, again my husband was moving all over the bed. This time I could actually see the indentation of a person sitting on the side of the bed.

Tamara

October 14th

 Room 301. I was awakened by a soft, moaning noise and a very strange smell in my room just around 3:00 a.m. and saw a fleeting shadow across the mirror by the window.

Lisa

October 15th

 Room 301. In the middle of the night I heard water running in the sink. My friend was asleep in the next bed, and no one was in the bathroom. My friend later heard noises that sounded like they were coming from inside the wall. She didn't want to wake me, and I didn't want to wake her.

Christine

October 18th

 Room 201. Every time we would come back to our room, we would find our door unlocked, even though we know we locked it.

Brandon

November 2nd

 Room 305. After settling into my room after check-in, I put my key on the desk and took a nap. When I was ready to leave, I went to get it and it was gone. I looked all over the room and checked my pockets, as well. The key was nowhere to be found. I went to the front desk and got another key so I could lock up my room, and then left for the day. I returned late last night and went right to bed. When I woke this morning, there was my key, right in the middle of the desktop.

No Name

November 2nd

 Room 209. All night long I had dreams of a woman trying to seduce me into bed. I kept trying to wake up but just couldn't do it. In the morning when I finally woke up, I could smell a very strong perfume in the air. After showering and dressing, just as I was leaving the room, I

heard a soft moan behind me. When I turned to look, I could clearly see
the image of a woman dressed in a black dress in the mirror.

No Name

November 4th

While touring the hotel, we were walking down the hall from
Room 412 toward 413 when we heard a music box playing. When we
told the front desk clerk about this, she said there was no one else on that
floor.

Gary

November 9th

I woke up in the middle of the night and noticed what I thought
was my boyfriend walking down the room's hall toward the door. He
appeared to be a figure in white. I started to ask him where he was going
in the middle of the night when I realized that he was still asleep next to
me.

Joy

November 11th

A young man claiming to be called
Jeremy Wilde (he specified the *E* at the end) -
he was sorrowful for killing "that girl."

Jesse

November 25th

Room 411. We had a very nice quiet
evening until we turned the lights out. Odd
things began to happen from what sounded
like the floor above us, yet we were on the top
floor. We could hear voices whispering to
one another. We could not make out what
they were saying, just a muffled whisper.
Then we heard what sounded like a trunk being pulled across the floor above. A very loud

voice said, "I have to do it." Then it sounded like someone closed the lid to the trunk. We turned the lights back on and the noise stopped. Yet when we turned them off, it started all over again, this time just the whispering from above. This went on until just after 3:00 a.m.

Jenn

December 8ᵗʰ

Room 314. We slept well, but at times I thought someone else was in the room with us. You could actually feel the presence of another person.

Dan & Carla

December 13ᵗʰ

I was about to fall asleep when a feeling of fear came over me. I felt a movement in the room at the foot of the bed. As I looked downward, I could see a dark figure, a form of a person. In a frightened state I sat up, and it seemed as if the form just watched me for a time, then just dissipated into the night.

Michael

December 28ᵗʰ

My husband Steve got up in the middle of the night to use the bathroom and get a drink of water. When he entered the bathroom and turned the light on, he noticed the mirror was moist and had fogged over. Just then my toothbrush fell off the counter, and the roll of toilet paper fell of the holder and rolled under the clawfoot tub. We see only one possible explanation for this metaphysical event, and it sends a deep chill through us, indeed.

Steve & Leslie

January 1, 2003

~

December 31, 2003

Copper Queen Hotel
Ghost Journal

January 3rd

Room 214. I had taken a shower, and the mirror had steamed up. While I brushed my hair, in the mirror I could definitely see the outline of a face and eyes that were looking back at me with a pleading look to them. Scared, I left the bathroom and returned about five minutes later. The image was gone, but the memory remains with me.

Sarah

January 5th

As we pulled up to the hotel to check in, my husband got out of the car along with our friend. I remained inside the car in the passenger seat as they went in to check in. A weird feeling suddenly washed over me. Then a few seconds later my husband started banging on the window and yelling for me to stop the car. I did not realize it at first, but the car was creeping slowly up the hill. I reached for the break but realized that the car was in *drive*. Someone or something had moved the shifter into *drive*. I shifted it back to *park*, and as I did that, a box of candy I had put in the console came flying onto my lap. We tested the car later on that evening to see what happened. We put the car in *drive* while we were on a hill, and it rolled backward, not forward like earlier this afternoon. So, even before we set foot into the hotel, we had an encounter.

Rhonda

January 28th
Room 315. Upon entering our room, the overhead light blew out, and suddenly there was an over whelming smell of perfume in the air. After a long day I went to sleep and around 3:00 a.m. I was awakened by a noise. Out of the corner of my eye to the right, I saw a woman leaning over and looking at the money I had left on the desk for the maids in the morning. This startled me. I yelled, and the woman disappeared.

No Name

February 8th
Room 307. We had left our TV on as we went out to do some shopping. Upon returning to our room, the TV had been turned off. I inquired at the desk if someone had been in our room and turned the TV off. The desk clerk informed me that other than the staff on the first floor, no one else was in the hotel. Our last night here I was awakened by a tap on my backside while sleeping in bed.

Mary

February 20th
Room 412. I had to leave the water run for a while for it to get hot for a shower. I could hear a small child crying while I was waiting. It was not until I was actually taking my shower that I realized the child I was hearing was coming from my bathroom.

Karen

February 23rd
Room 318. Just after midnight we heard loud thumping out in the

hall. When I checked, there was nothing and no one there. This continued to happen on and off until about 1:30 a.m.

No Name

March 4th

Room 401. There were four of us in this room. I was in the bathroom, washing my hands. Suddenly, the lid on the toilet slammed down, and I heard "tee hee hee" very faintly.

Dorma

March 15th

Room 201. We were awakened from a deep sleep at 3:00 a.m. to the noise of what sounded like a dozen or more people talking in the hall just outside our door. After about five minutes of this, I got up to ask them to quiet down or move someplace else; however, when I opened the door, there was no one there. This went on for about thirty minutes.

Dan & Cindy

March 16th

Room 312. I had a peaceful night, other than waking up in the middle of the night at 3:10 a.m. and hearing a book sliding across the nightstand. I thought it was my uncle John in the other bed; however, when I checked, I found he was sound asleep. The next morning when I woke up, the book that was on the nightstand in between the beds was now on the desk across the room.

Ron

March 21st

Our first night here I saw a figure, white and tall, in the stairwell between the 1st and 2nd floor. It was there and gone in a flash. Also, as I sat down on the bed in our room, I saw what looked like a black firefly floating next to me. I found it rather impossible to sleep both of our nights here. I kept waking up every few minutes with a very unsettling feeling as if someone else was in the room. Despite this, I loved the charming hotel with all of its history in the quirky, lovely town of Bisbee.

Marcy

> P.S. My friend asked me, as she was standing directly
> beside me, if I "tapped" her on the leg. I did not and we
> were alone.

March, 26th

Room 312. As I entered the bathroom, the first thing I noticed was that the clothes I had left folded on the counter were strewn all about the floor. As I bent over to pick them up with wonderment at how this occurred, the bathroom door closed behind me, and I heard the pitter-patter of feet along with a childish laugh. Then the door to my room opened and closed.

Sydney

March 27th

Room 312. After checking in and unpacking my things, I decided to take a shower. Approximately two minutes after starting my shower, the makeup box I had set on the counter in the bathroom fell to the floor. Not giving this much thought, I went about my day. The next morning I had set a cup of hot coffee on the same counter to cool as I took my morning shower, and it also mysteriously fell to the floor.

Audrey

April 18th

Normally I'm a very sound sleeper. My sister informed me that all through the night I tossed and turned and repeated the words, "No, No, No." She also said I cried for quite some time in my sleep.

Margie

April 27th

Room 409. While using the bathroom, I heard a slight moaning, kind of like a whimper, come from the corner of the room. When I looked up, I saw the window curtain move. I checked and the window was closed tight without any breeze coming through.

Stephanie

May 18th

Room 301. Late in the night we heard the cry of not a child but of an adult, loud enough to wake us from our sleep. It started in the hallway and came floating through the room. It was very hard to determine its source since it seemed as if it came from the window one second and then from the ceiling or hall the next.

No Name

May 27th

The drawer in the nightstand opened and the handle banged downward just as we were about to fall asleep. It was dark, but we both heard it.

No Name

May 27th

Room 203. When I looked at my watch, I was shocked to see that we were twenty minutes past the check-out time. It seemed impossible. I checked the room clock, and it turned out my watch was precisely two hours ahead of the real time. When I asked my husband if he messed with my watch, he said, "No, how could I? It's been on your arm the whole time," which of course was true.

Diane

June 18th

Room 318. I was resting on the bed, watching TV for about an hour before dinner. There was periodically what I though was a luggage cart or a trunk being pulled down the hall to bring luggage to new guests arriving to stay. After about the fifth time, I was getting upset that so much noise was made for newly arriving guests. I then got up because it was just too noisy to watch TV any more, and went to dinner. Hearing the noise of the luggage cart or trunk when I left the room, I anticipated seeing more people in the hallway. I was astonished that there was not a soul in the hallway. After dinner I stopped to chat with the front desk clerk and asked about the luggage cart and all the people checking in. She informed me that they did not even have a luggage cart and that I was the only person staying in that hallway. She did, however, tell me that they get a lot of reports from people hearing the same type of things that I did.

Susan

June 23rd

We were just visiting the hotel, and as we came to the top of the stairs on the 4th floor, we noticed the front window was open and a cool breeze was coming through. We walked the floor, and on our way back down noticed that the window had been closed and that there was what seemed to be a foggy form of a man in the mirror on the wall.

Austin

July 3rd

Room 315. Staying here at the hotel is great. We decided to take some pictures of ourselves in our room using a digital camera. I took several pictures of my husband and they turned out just fine, no blurs or anything. After taking a few pictures of me, we noticed that each picture had some sort of orb in it; one was right next to me on the couch.

Steve & Linda

July 10th

Not able to sleep, I decided to go out to the 3rd floor balcony and have a smoke. After being there for about five minutes, I noticed a man at the other end of the balcony, smoking a cigar. I had not noticed him when I arrived. I turned to set my water down and was going to go over and say *hi* to this gentleman, but when I turned back around, he was gone. The door to the balcony is loud, and I did not hear it open and close.

Middy

July 12th

Room 316. About 4:00 a.m. I felt something pushing on my

shoulders. I looked up and saw a fog in the shape of a woman. I could not sleep the rest of the night.

Jon

July 12ᵗʰ

After a day of sightseeing, we decided to head back to our room and freshen up for dinner. After brushing my teeth and dressing, I returned to the bathroom to brush my hair. Right on the vanity was a lock of black hair that was not there before. I found this to be a little odd since both my husband and I have white hair.

Anna

July 13ᵗʰ

Room 310. We had nightmares like crazy all night long. We heard knocking and something being dragged across the floor. My husband dreamt about a murder of a man named Fred. I was yelling in my sleep all night according to my husband.

No Name

July 13ᵗʰ

Room 315. From the moment we arrived I felt a presence in our room. At one point the green glass lampshade on the desk changed positions. After taking some pictures, we noticed a white fog on some of them, one over the sofa and then again over the desk. All of the other pictures we took in and out of the hotel were fine.

Bob

July 20ᵗʰ

While taking a shower in the morning, I heard what sounded like a door opening but decided to dismiss it at that moment. Then suddenly, I felt a whoosh of cool air, and the shower curtain moved. I quickly pulled the curtain open, and no one was there. The doors to my room and to the bathroom were both closed.

Fernando

July 29th

　　Room 409. I was taking a shower and I had left the TV on. Suddenly, the TV went off. Being in the shower and soaking wet, I decided to let it go. Then I heard a very deep voice, like a mumbling. Not able to make out what he was saying, I decided it was time to get out of the shower and get out of the room. After turning off the water, it came back on for a few seconds and then went off again.

Carl

August 14th

　　Room 312. We thoroughly enjoyed our stay. Last night all through the night we heard noises from the bathroom, drawers opening and closing, even dripping water at one time. Twice we noticed that the bathroom door changed positions – at one point it was closed, and a few hours later it was halfway open.

Elise

August 18th

　　We had a great stay here at the Copper Queen Hotel. We will be back. Both nights of our stay around 3:00 a.m., it sounded like someone was standing outside our door playing with change, like tossing coins from one hand to the other and back again. This went on for about an hour.

Shannon

August 26th

　　While in the restroom, something touched the back of my neck.

No Name

September 5th

　　I received a call at the front desk at approximately 1:00 a.m. from Room 305, saying there was a loud clicking noise coming from the room next door. This would be Room 306, but it was empty. I went up to check on the noise and did hear a clicking type of noise come from the room. As I opened the door, it abruptly stopped. No sooner had I returned to the front desk that Room 305 called asking if I was going to check to see what was causing this noise, as she could not sleep. I told her I went up already and that the noise had stopped. She explained that it was happening as we spoke and asked me to come back upstairs. When I got to the 3rd floor, the woman from 305 was standing outside her door, waiting for me. Again as soon as I opened the door, the noise stopped. But this time just as I shut the door, it started back up again. The woman from 305 asked if she could be moved to a different room. I accommodated her wish and even moved her to a different floor.

Front Desk Clerk - No Name

September 9th

     I was awakened by the sound of a zipper. Thinking that my husband was already awake and getting dressed for the day, I turned over in bed and was surprised to find him sound asleep right next to me.

Rhonda

September 12th

     I heard a faint knocking on the wall and felt a presence in the room all night long.

Chris

September 14th

     While standing in the hall-way where the Saloon and bath-rooms are and reading the articles in the display case, I could see the re-flections of people walking behind me. I noticed that a gentleman had stopped and was looking over my shoulder, reading the same thing I was. He looked like a very nice person, so I turned to say *hello,* and there was no one there.

Marisa

September 20th

Room 201. What an experience for us! This was our first time, as well as it was for our two grandsons, ages six and eight. Thank you for taking me back in time to Grandma's house. The boys didn't want to leave (me either). We'll be back.

Julie and Joe

September 21st

Room 312. My stuffed animal was on my pillow when I left my room. When I came back, he was at the end of my bed.

Erin

September 26th

Room 206. I was awakened at 3:00 a.m. by a banging and thumping noise coming from the closet. Unsettled by this, I got up and investigated but of course, nothing and no one was there. Try as I might, I was in and out of sleep the rest of the night.

No Name

September 28th

I don't know about the hotel, but Room 317 is definitely haunted.

No Name

September 29th

Room 311. Something happened last night. Our candle flickered every time we closed our eyes. When we opened them, it would stop. Also, our half bottle of wine that was in our cooler bag was uncorked and disposed of.

Eric

October 1st

Room 205. We were awakened at 3:00 a.m. and again at 4:00 a.m. to the sounds of commotion and what sounded like a party going on in the courtyard below our room. Each time we looked out, there was nothing going on and not a person around.

No Name

October 7th

Room 310. When we arrived, the flags on the balcony outside our room were tangled and wrapped around the flagpoles. We untangled them and had them unraveled and hanging free. There was little to no wind during the night, but the flags were once again wrapped around the flagpoles in the morning. The flag on the west side was especially tightly wrapped. Also, at 4:00 a.m. there was a licorice cigar smoke smell wafting into our room from the balcony.

No Name

October 9th

Room 217. I heard the sounds of little children running and laughing in the hallway at 12:00 midnight and again at 2:00 a.m. Both times I checked the hallway and saw no one at all.

No Name

October 12th

Room 315. Both my fiancé and I have small overnight kits, mine with my make up and his with his shaving equipment. Both of our kits were sitting side by side on the sink. At 12:30 a.m. we were awakened by a noise in the bathroom. My fiancé went to check and see what happened and found that my kit had fallen off the counter. He replaced it and then returned to bed. No more than a half an hour later at 1:00 a.m. the same noise occurred. He checked again, and again my kit was knocked off the counter with all of the contents strewn about the floor. Why just me?

No Name

October 15th

Room 209. Your ghost kept pulling down my sheets! It was a warm night even with our fan on. Thank you, everyone for a fun-filled visit. Hope to return very soon.

Savanna & Stony

October 19th
    Room 406. Great stay! A little scary but great.

Jay & Marion

October 22nd
    No ghost experiences, darn. I was ready for them, too. Great hotel.

No Name

October 24th
    Room 406. Heard clanking outside of our room. The sound went up and down the hallway from 3:00 a.m. to 4:00 a.m. It sounded like someone walking with spurs on.

Brian

October 31st
    Room 406. Our son left a toy out for the "little boy" to play with. Every time we checked on it, it had been moved or flipped over.

Natalie

November 2nd
    We heard two people on the street between the hotel and the museum at about 2:00 a.m. I looked over the balcony to see who might be out there at this time of the morning. I could not see anyone. The male voice said, "I love you. Come back to bed." The woman was crying, and then it all just faded away.

Marie

November 7th

Room 311. Waited for the ghost, but nobody showed up.

Betty

November 10th

Room 315. No ghost. Julia didn't show up.

Annette & Al

November 16th

Room 311. On our way out to dinner, I set my reading glasses on the nightstand next to the bed. Upon returning to our room a few hours later, my glasses had been moved from the nightstand to on top of my pillow.

Deborah

November 19th

Excellent restaurant and piano music in the Saloon! No ghosts, but we enjoyed our stay.

Lori & Tom

November 21st

Mark and Diane stayed one night for Diane's birthday. Fun place. However, no spirits observed this time.

Mark & Diane

November 23rd

Room 401. We really enjoyed our stay, coming from Gilbert, Arizona. My daughter felt someone pull on her foot the first night, and saw a shadowy figure of a woman in the mirror the second night.

Nancy & Tania

November 28th

     Room 411. I was awakened at 2:00 a.m. by a childlike humming in the corner of my room.

No Name

November 28th

     Room 409. Just prior to going to bed, we noticed a very strong cigar smoke smell overtake the room. Opening the windows to air out the room, we were able to fall asleep until a noise woke us at 2:00 a.m. The windows were closed, and you could see a shadow of a person moving across the ceiling.

Emily & Lauren

November 28th

     Room 314. A very restless night.

Bill

November 29th

     I was looking for the tweezers my mom had set on the nightstand; I remember her putting them there. As my mom took her bath, I decided to brush my hair. I dropped my brush, and there were the tweezers under the desk. How?

No Name

December 10th

     I had no ghostly experiences this time. However, I had two very restful nights of sleep. Strangely though, I had two vivid dreams about a person I had not thought of for over six years. I wonder....

Spencer

December 17th

     Room 315. I don't have much to describe, except for what I thought happened between the awake state and sleep. We were lying in our bed, watching television, when we felt the bed move with a sudden shudder. I shot up in bed, noted the time (it was 9:32 p.m.) and looked out the window. It felt as if someone had shut a door hard and vibrated the wall along with the bed. As a skeptic, I went back to bed (tossing and turning) and explored our surroundings. I noted that the very wall our bed was on found the outside, so the shudder did not originate from someone in the next room slamming a door. I checked the exit outside our room leading to the pool and noted that it doesn't shut unless pulled.

Jane

December 29th

My husband and I had turned out the light, said good night and settled down for a comfy rest, when I smelled the very strong aroma of cigar smoke. I said to my husband, "I thought this was a non-smoking room!" I smelled the blanket, but the odor was not there. It was only in the air and smelled fresh like someone was in the room smoking. I went to the front desk the next morning to complain, and that is when I learned about the older gentleman who smokes a good cigar on the 4th floor. What fun.

Judith

December 29th

Room 210. Asleep in the middle of the night, I felt my head being pressed down into the pillow. I could not lift it up and off the pillow for a number of minutes. I tried to raise my head a number of times and could only get it about a foot in the air. This went on for about ten minutes.

Matt

January 1, 2004

~

December 31, 2004

Copper Queen Hotel
Ghost Journal

January 3rd

Room 303, I felt a little freaked out when we first checked into the hotel. I could feel something but could not figure out what it was that was bothering me. After going to bed I found that I needed to go to the bathroom yet I was afraid to get out of bed. At 12:30am I heard what sounded like a child running up and down the hallway laughing. I had very vivid dreams about a place between heaven and hell.

Jennifer

January 4th

Room 307. Very late at night something woke me, and I heard someone playing an instrument similar to a juice harp (twangs). Felt a presence in the room from that point forward.

Martha

January 6ᵗʰ

 Room 406. We checked in during the day and found no suspicious activity. Around 10:00 p.m. my mom and I were walking around the hotel taking pictures. When we got back to our room, I recorded a short clip on my camera of my mom talking to any ghosts in our room. (We saw it done on a TV show). When I played it back, there was a light in the mirror my mom was standing next to that took the form of a woman's face. You could actually see it moving on the video. We tried to go to sleep but couldn't; every time my mom almost got to sleep, she felt something push her awake. I was lying next to her and felt her body jerk. I couldn't sleep because I kept getting the feeling someone was watching us. My sister was also awake because she felt tapping on her leg.

The Brawn girls

January 7ᵗʰ

 We had a great stay in the John Wayne room, but I did not sense any paranormal activity.

Cristie

January 18ᵗʰ

 I met Charlie Sheen in the restaurant yesterday while we were having lunch, after which we toured the town on the trolley. It was spectacular. At some point during the evening, as I slept having a dream, I was awakened and my eyes popped open to someone saying, "I'm available. I'm ready to drift before you. Just put some copper pennies into my hand."

Meg

January 30ᵗʰ

 Dear Innkeeper,

 I had a wonderful, peaceful stay and enjoyed historic Bisbee. This town and hotel are just beautiful. Thanks for the gracious hospitality, the delicious food and my lovely room. Just no ghosts.

Eva

February 10th

No ghosts but had a great stay. The hotel has a wonderful, old world charm, and Bisbee is a great delight.

Randolph

February 12th

Room 310. Had a great time. Did not believe in the ghost stories about this hotel. Never saw a ghost before in my life. I went to bed around 10:00 p.m. and was sleeping peacefully when I suddenly woke up and saw the image of a female hovering above me. Totally scared, I yelled and closed my eyes. When I reopened them, the image was gone and all that was there was the ceiling fan.

Nathan

February 19th

We stayed in Room 409 and think we may have had extra company. The bathroom door kept opening and closing very slowly. Great room and hotel.

Lillian

February 20th

At 2:30 a.m., heard two people breathing, and there was only one other person in room. For some reason it sounded like a woman.

Jake

February 27ᵗʰ

My brother and I were sharing Room 402, with my parents across the hallway. When we went to bed, I had left my watch on the dresser. In the morning it was on the floor.

Mark

February 29ᵗʰ

Tried but just couldn't sleep last night for all the noise! Kept hearing walking/running down the hall outside our room. Also, heard a giggling sound at 3:20 a.m. and a loud bang through the floor that shook my bed.

Michelle

February 29ᵗʰ

Room 406. As I was washing my face, something hit me. I thought my husband was playing around and threw something at me. We realized it was the cap from the faucet that flew off and hit me. They are very hard to get off even with a screwdriver. In the morning the window shade sprung up, and my husband felt something brush his back. Thinking I did it, he turned around and found that I was in the bathroom.

Jay & Barbara

March 3ʳᵈ

We stayed in Room 318 for a number of days. On the last day I woke up to clean up and check out. Nothing happened on our stay except for today, the very last day of our stay. I swore that I had left my eyeglasses on the night stand on my side of the bed when we went to sleep. When I woke up to clean up, my eyeglasses were found on the floor on the opposite side of the bed near the other nightstand.

Liz

March 4ᵗʰ

    Nope, no ghosts, but had a superb time. Great entertainment in the Saloon and great food in Winchester's.

                      Lawrence

March 18ᵗʰ

    Room 409. Relaxing and watching TV, we started to smell cigar smoke coming into our room. It seemed like someone was smoking in the hall right outside our room. I went to the hallway to see if someone was smoking, and there was no one there. I went down to the front desk and asked them to check it out. When we got back upstairs, you could not smell anything, like no one had smoked at all.

                                         Alex

March 22ⁿᵈ

    Good food, good coffee, nice room, wonderful weather, and friendly staff. HOWEVER, WE SAW NO GHOSTS. DARN IT.

                             Joanne & Jerry

April 4ᵗʰ

    My husband was scared to death!!! He heard a noise. We had lots of fun. Thanks for everything.

                                   Stephanie

April 10th

When we woke up in the morning, we found my hairbrush on the floor in the middle of the room.

Pat

April 19th

As we were walking back to the door to the pool to go back to our room, the door started to open on its own, almost like inviting us back into the hotel. But know one was there.

Cindy

April 24th

After a long day of visiting the shops in town and having had a great dinner, it was time for sleep. Just prior to going to bed, I locked all three locks on our door. In the morning on our way out, I noticed that only one lock remained locked.

Marjorie

April 29th

When we arrived in town, we knew nothing about this hotel. Unloading our luggage, I noticed a black shadow go across the front steps. A second later the shadow re-emerged, and this time it looked like that of a man in a black coat and wearing a top hat.

Darla

May 4th

Thank you for an amazing, romantic visit.

Barb

May 11ᵗʰ

Room 315. Woke up in the middle of the night to the sound of someone breathing about an inch away from my ear. I held my breath in case it was just me. But the whistling nostril and breathing continued.

Karen

May 16ᵗʰ

Room 312. We were expecting or should I say hoping for a visitor and had none. Beautiful stay as always.

The Trubees

May 21ˢᵗ

Room 315. At 9:00 a.m. this morning the construction guys in the room above mine made a perpetual din of noise for over an hour. They dragged chairs, dropped things and carried on a loud conversation. I was trying to sleep in and was very annoyed. Later I asked the front desk what kind of renovation was being done in that room. The front desk clerk said that there wasn't any. Not only that, but there were no registered occupants in a room above me.

Karen

May 27ᵗʰ

Room 402. Needing to check out early in the morning at about 4:00 a.m. we left our room and headed for the elevator around the corner. Both my wife and I saw a gentleman behind us when we got to the corner of the hallway. We both turned to say *good morning* and to ask if he had to leave early, as well. When we looked behind us to talk to him, he was gone.

Steve

June 12ᵗʰ

We had a great time. We wanted to have a ghostly experience but are probably lucky we didn't. Great hotel.

Darcy

June 18ᵗʰ

Room 403. I was awakened by the feel of someone sleeping beside me, their legs touching mine. I was alone but could feel the presence. About a half an hour later still laying awake, I noticed the form of a woman to the left of my bed. She was older yet very beautiful, dressed in flowing clothes with a lace shawl over her head. She moved around the bed to the right side, keeping an eye on me with every move. It appeared there were people reaching for her the way she moved. There was a soft glow, a light of some sort illuminating her. I reached out and she disappeared. I don't know why, but I felt very calm and started to drift off to sleep, when I suddenly felt an arm reach around my shoulders. I could actually feel the weight of the arm. When I turned, there was no one or should I say nothing there. Needless to say, I didn't get much sleep.

Kathy

June 22ⁿᵈ

Great stay, but no ghost.

The Aussie

July 15ᵗʰ

Having arrived here from the United Kingdom, we stayed in Room 210, not being believers in ghosts. However, during the night you could definitely feel that there was someone else in the room with us –

small noises, and the lamp itself turned on and off a number of times through the night, waking us up.

Robert

July 21ˢᵗ

    Room 311. After being warned ghosts might make their presence known, every sound had great significance. Nothing unusual in the way of sounds happened. However, I woke up in the middle of the night and was aware someone was pushing me, causing me to hold firm. The pressure felt hard enough to slide to the other side of the bed! As a result, I was a bit afraid to leave my bed until morning, no matter how badly I needed to use the restroom. Great room. Loved our stay.

Harriet

July 24ᵗʰ

    Room 204. After shutting and locking the door to my room, I showered and prepared to go out for the day. Ready to leave, I found my door unlocked and open. Every picture we took inside the hotel was blurry and contained hazy spots, but the pictures we took everyplace else were just fine.

Chelsie

July 27ᵗʰ

    Room 409. At about 2:15 a.m. my father got out of bed, and upon his return a small round light was shining in the middle of his side of the bed. He looked up to see where the light (about the size of a pencil eraser tip) was coming from. There was nothing on the ceiling other than an air conditioning vent with no such pattern on it. He laid back on the bed over the light and had a restful night sleep thereafter. At daylight we looked all over the room for some explanation and found even the vent was off to the side of the bed. There was no explanation at all for how or why the light was there.

Jan

August 3rd

I was walking down the steps from the 3rd floor to the 2nd floor, and I heard, from behind me, extra footstep sounds. Halfway down the last set of stairs, I turned around and saw absolutely nobody. I have never been to this hotel -- it's my first visit -- and had no idea about the stories of ghosts here.

Charles Cordova

August 5th

We were eating dinner out on the front porch when our wine container that was on the floor mysteriously fell over. We are convinced that it was the work of one of the ghosts since no one touched it, there was no wind, and the bottle had been resting "uphill."

Bob & Linda

August 13th

Thanks for a great time.

Frank & Sandy

August 15th

We did not see nor hear any spirits, just had some unusual dreams and sweet sleep. Had a pleasant time.

Rita

August 17th

Woke up to find the bathroom light had been turned on. I am here alone and thought I had turned it off. I turned the light off and then went back to bed, only to awake in the morning to find the light was back on.

No Name

August 24th

Room 404. We smelled the cigar smoke outside of our room for about two minutes. We sensed his presence, but no visual.

Terry & Becky

August 24th

What a wonderful way to spend an anniversary! The only thing that would have made our stay more memorable would have been to see a ghost. Oh well, maybe next time.

Grant & Diane

August 25th

My family and I were eating dinner when the waiter brought out my lemonade. I was playing with the lemon on the glass, and then we all started to have a conversation. When I went to grab my drink, it was clear across the table! Everyone swore they didn't touch it.

Abby

August 26th

Someone got into the elevator just as we walked up. The elevator had not started up, so we pushed the button to get on. When the door reopened, no one was there except the faint smell of a cigar.

No Name

September 7th

Room 404. We enjoyed our stay. I did wake up to the sweet smell of a cigar. My husband admitted the next morning he also woke to the smell of a cigar.

Jean

September 11th

I was using the bathroom when I heard what sounded like a woman's voice. It was whispering and sounded like she said, "Is that you?" I was the only one in the room.

Margo

September 13th

Room 409. OK, so I really don't believe in anything supernatural. Go figure, we check in and I go up to get ready for dinner. I close the door and lock it. Suddenly, the lights went off and the bathroom door slammed shut.

No Name

September 18th

I smelled the cigar smoke outside the Teddy Roosevelt Room. I had to leave the floor when I saw a blurry figure on the hallway.

Gregory

September 20ᵗʰ

     Room 406. Last night was the first time we stayed here. My friend and I were in the room, and the fan went off all by itself shortly after we got there. While watching the TV in the morning, it also just turned off. However, the strangest was hearing a woman singing at 4:00 a.m. We were both awake and heard her. Sweet sounds, but didn't understand the words or tune.

Nancy

September 25ᵗʰ

     Room 212. We were awakened in the middle of the night by the feeling of a presence in the room. We saw a young woman standing near the window. It was very unnerving. Later everything returned to normal.

Ann

September 25th

Room 295. Last night my girlfriend and I walked up to the 2nd and 3rd floor. On the 3rd floor we smelled the sweet smell of a cigar. It was a pleasant smell. On the 2nd floor I felt a presence of someone close by. I took about four or five steps, and it felt as if it got stronger. The hair on the back of my neck stood up. I was not scared but felt my body temperature drop, and then the feeling went away.

Robert & Sandy

October 4th

Room 312. Due to the wife, we slept with the lights on!!! Quiet night. Nothing happened.

Tom

October 5th

Room 211. In the morning as I was getting out of the shower, I noticed there was some kind of writing in the steam on the mirror. Billy?

Byrd & Hank

October 5th

We spent our first wedding anniversary here at the Copper Queen and are having a wonderful time. We will be back, ghosts and all.

Joel & Jeannine

October 7th

Room 315. We were awakened at 1:30 a.m. by the laughter of a small child. Someone whispered "toys" in my wife's ear. We checked, and there were no small children staying in the hotel.

George & Elona

October 9th

Well, we didn't have the ghostly experience we were looking for; however, I could swear there was a cat in the room while I was sleeping. Maybe there are ghost cats. We had a great time.

The Stewarts

October 13th

Enjoyed the Copper Queen Hotel once again. It's like coming home to see family since my husband's family did start here. Thank you for the great food.

Chuck & Beth

October 18th

Room 309. I was walking around at a quarter to one o'clock in the morning, listening to my walkman. I stopped on the 2nd floor and decided to relax on the sofa and jam with my walkman. I closed my eyes and got lost in my music. Next thing I knew, someone or something pulled the back of my hair, hard too. I jumped up so fast you would have thought I was the ghost. I was gone, outa here.

No Name

October 22nd

Room 310. Last night we were exploring when we heard a strange sound and then saw a flash of light in the hallway. No one was around.

Nicole

October 24th

    Room 406. Sunday morning my husband was in the bathroom, and two different times a single coin fell onto the floor from no apparent source.

No Name

October 24th

    Room 210. When I was trying to fall asleep about 11:30 p.m., every five seconds I would hear a clicking sound, like keys banging. Sometimes it would happen two times in a row. You could also hear people talking in the hallway. When I went out to the hall to check, there was no one there.

Hannah

October 25th

    Room 315. We so enjoyed our stay at the Copper Queen. Our first night we heard the sound of shuffling papers in the desk area of our room. Also, there were what sounded like creaking sounds on the floor, like someone walking around the room all night long. There was also the sound of a yowling cat outside the window. The second night was quiet except for the smell of tobacco for a short while. We are looking forward to coming back soon.

Doris & Joe

October 31st

    Room 212. At about 12:30 a.m. I felt someone snuggled up behind me, even though my husband was on the other side of me. I tried to move the covers back and couldn't. I tried to rise but felt strangely pinned down, but not uncomfortably so. I then moved over to my husband and got up. Nothing was to be seen, but I slept the rest of the night with the lights on.

Kerrie

November 7th

Room 211. Last night when my husband and I went to sleep, we had pulled all of the window shades down. By morning the one shade behind my head had been put all the way up. We heard nothing, and we are light sleepers.

Amy

November 14th

Room 208. I woke up during the night several times hearing what I thought was my husband getting up and walking across the room to the bathroom. Each time I looked over and my husband was still sound asleep. Clearly, there was the noise and sense of someone moving about.

Patty

November, 20th

The girls and I came to Bisbee hoping to see the ghosts. At one point the coffee cups and the menu were knocked off the TV in our room. Not only that, but we could feel the presence of the ghosts the entire time we were here. It was kind of comforting, not scary.

No Name

November 20th

Our first time here. Great staff, great food, great room, great ambience.

Rob & Debbie

November 23rd

Room 312. This was our first night here. While watching TV late at night, I looked up and noticed the ceiling fan was moving around very slowly. I thought the windows were open and the breeze was making the fan move. Upon checking, I found the windows were definitely closed.

No Name

November 23rd

Room 401. While we were playing cards, the lights flickered constantly. My husband went to the front desk to see if there was a problem or a storm outside. No problems and no storm. The lights went back to normal as soon as we were done playing cards.

Jill

November 26th

Room 313. While sitting on the second floor talking with friends, we heard a very loud bang from around the corner. When we ran to check, we found no one and nothing there. Throughout the night we heard banging in the hall and rattling of our door handle. Around 3:00 a.m. we were awakened when a glass fell off the back of the toilet and shattered. You could definitely feel a presence throughout the night.

James

November 27th

Room 412. Sometime in the middle of the night my shirt was moved from one end of the room to the other.

Jack

November 30th

Room 307, 5:26 a.m. While we were just laying in bed relaxing and thinking about the day ahead, our smoke detector went off for about five seconds.

Kathy

November 30th

Room 305. My boyfriend heard a drilling sound in the middle of the night just outside our door. We checked and there was nothing there.

Bonnie

December 7th

Room 401. I felt the sheet being pulled out from under my body while I was lying in bed. Jumping out of bed to see what the heck was happening, I found my sheets were just fine. It just seemed so real.

No Name

December 21st

Room 409. During the evening my husband was almost asleep when he jumped up off the bed and said, "I was almost asleep, and something pulled on my thumb and index finger and startled me awake." Later in the night my mother was asleep when she was pushed /turned gently onto her side. It woke her up and she told me what happened, then went back to sleep. I loved every minute of it.

Silvia

December 22nd

Room 406. At 5:00 a.m. I heard a male speaking Spanish and laughing. Then I felt a person lay next to me in bed. My brother heard the commotion and moved near me. I felt a cold breeze, and the body moved off my bed.

No Name

December 23rd

I asked my husband if I could use his ChapStick, and he said, "Sure, it's in my pocket." Well, I looked and it wasn't there. He was so sure it was. We looked high and low for it. Finally, it showed up in my cosmetic bag. We did not put it there.

Wilma

December 28th

Room 409. The heater was going on and off all night long. The thing is, we had turned the heater off before we went to bed. We also heard knocking at the door to our room, and when we checked, no one was there.

Bettie

December 29th

Room 210. Last night I remember the door of the bathroom being closed and the lights off. As I drifted off to sleep, I could hear the dogs barking and the skateboarders outside. Early in the morning I heard footsteps and the creaking of the floor. I thought nothing of it and went back to sleep. This morning when I woke up, the bathroom door was open and the light was on. No one had gone into the bathroom all night.

Megan

January 1, 2005

~

December 31, 2005

Copper Queen Hotel
Ghost Journal

January 5th

     While we were sitting quietly watching TV, the bottom part of the lamp in the room turned on all by itself. We decided not to turn it off.

No Name

January 17th

     Room 301. Shortly after my grandfather turned on the water to take a shower, I heard a high-pitched scream come from the bathroom. I ran in to check on him, and he was standing there brushing his teeth. He said he hadn't said a word.

No Name

January 20th

Room 312. I was sleeping peacefully when I was awakened by a soft moaning sound in the far corner of the room. I tried to go back to sleep but only tossed and turned. Sometime past 2:00 a.m. I heard a small child crying, followed by, "Over here, Mommy."

David

January 20th

Although I can't say I believe in ghosts, I do believe in psychic energy. I had numerous dreams over the past two nights of people and places I don't even know. Normally, I sleep very soundly but not in this hotel.

No Name

January 23rd

Room 301. We were here for two nights. The first night was a nice quiet night, no happenings. The second night, not the same. I heard what sounded like a person walking around the room all night. I kept drifting off to sleep, but at 2:15 a.m. I was wide awake as I heard the sound of the door handle to our room moving. I sat up in bed and noticed the figure of a man standing by the window.

No Name

January 24th

Room 313. I know absolutely that I put the chain on the door before I went to bed last night, only to wake up this morning with it off. I never heard a sound. My toothbrush is also missing.

K.P.

January 25th

Room 312. We heard heavy footsteps walking across the room on the floor above us, to the point of having to call the front desk to call the room and ask them to quiet down. We were informed that no one was in the room above us.

No Name

January 27th

We walked into the lob-by. You could feel them all around.

Jan

January 29th

Room 412. During the night I heard a huge bang and then footsteps running down the hallway extremely fast. It seemed to stop just past our door. We all heard clicking noises coming from down the hall but had no idea what it was. In the morning we found our door unlocked.

The Ricci Family

February 3rd

There's an old guy that sits in the corner chair. He decided when it was time for me to go. He walked me to my room.

Marilyn

February 5th

We enjoyed our stay at the Copper Queen and were pleasantly surprised to not have any uninvited guests. Heater made mysterious noises all night, but kept us very warm. Thanks for the hospitality and the great restaurant dinner that we had.

D. Vermillion

February 13th

Room 307. The smell of cigar smoke was in the room, then went away as fast as it came. The second whiff of cigar smoke came in much stronger. I then said, "Hello," and the cigar smoke went away. The next morning I came to read the registry and found that many people had smelled the cigar smoke. Great fun!

RJ & Theresa

February 14th

Thanks for the great hospitality. Hope to come back again. We did capture several "orb" shots on the digital cameras. It was fun.

Greg

February 20th

Room 406. This evening, as we relaxed upon the bed (the one on the north side), I felt my legs suddenly drop, as though someone had sat down on the bottom edge of the bed. I looked but saw nothing. I tried to relax, but it happened again. Someone or something was forcing the lower edge of the bed down, which I could feel as my lower legs dropped. This happened three times with no explanation.

No Name

February 20th

Room 314.   Yes, there are "GHOSTS." Be aware of a "wake-up call" at 3:14 a.m.

The Warners

February 23rd

Room 406. We felt the presence of the older gentleman ghost. It was eerie! We were surrounded by the aroma of his cigar all night.

Maureen

February 26th

Billy visited our room this morning. We only could find one key and looked everywhere for the second one. After a while it "magically" appeared in plain sight under the chair. We also heard giggling during the night.

The Costich Family

February 28th

Room 316. Around 2:00 a.m. a real strong, sweet perfume smell appeared twice in our room.

Sid

March 8th

Room 309. Heard tapping sound at 5:30 a.m. It sounded like Morse code.

Diane

March 12th

  Best stay ever!!! Would stay longer if possible.

The Newmans

March 13th

  Room 313. At 6:30 a.m. I took a shower and the hot water was fine. At 7:10 a.m. my husband tried to take a shower and the hot water would not come on except for a trickle in the tub, but worked fine in the sink. . I guess the ghost thought he needed a cold shower.

Bob & Toni

March 13th

  Room 208. When we woke up this morning, my husband's shoes were placed against the door leading out to the hallway. The shoes were obviously placed in a position that was unmistakably done by someone last night while we were sleeping.

Bonnie & Rich

March 16th

  Room 413. At about 3:00 a.m. I woke up and saw a dark shadow figure in front of the bathroom door. It went away quickly.

No Name

March 16th

  Room 310. We heard footsteps on the balcony out front at 3:50 a.m. and 4:10 a.m. Both times we checked out front and saw no one.

Red

March 17th

Room 312. Nothing really happened; however, all night long we felt a presence in the room. At one point it felt as if someone was playing with my hair.

Kira

March 19th

Room 210. Just after we turned off the lights, about fifteen minutes later we heard a sliding sound, like books on a shelf. The sound came from the window area. We also saw a bright white flash on the wall above the TV. We're coming back for sure.

The Johnsons

March 19th

Room 318. The first of two nights of our stay -- no sounds, just a soft glow near the ceiling above the dresser, which came and went a couple of times. Also, a cool breeze, stronger than the fan which was on low and a brief increase in weight on the bed spread. The radium dial on my wrist watch on the table beside the bed had an extra bright glow. The energy was very high this evening.

Bill & Virginia

March 20th

Room 411. At about 3:00 a.m. our phone message light went on. Startled and unsure, I listened to the message on the phone. It was from a woman I didn't know. She said it was 7:30 a.m. and it was time to meet. When I checked with the front desk, the clerk said there had been no incoming calls.

Jim

March 20th

We had a strange experience that happened around midnight. My husband was asleep, and I had just turned off all the lights and the TV. Attempting to go to sleep, I felt someone sit on the end of the bed and stroke my feet. I immediately sat up but didn't see anything.

Dell & Jerry

March 26th

Room 401. I awoke to the smell of cigar smoke at about 2:00 a.m., looked to the side of my bed and noticed the dark image of a gentleman sitting at the desk by the door. Shortly after, I fell asleep again but was awakened once again by the smell of the cigar. This time no one was there.

Erin

March 30th

Room 214. We received the key and promptly went to our room. The second we entered I felt uncomfortable and felt some kind of presence in the room, deciding to move rooms we chose Room 216. At 3:15 a.m. I was awakened by the sound of a little boy crying. It only lasted a minute or two and then stopped. We had a fabulous time at the Copper Queen and Bisbee.

Barbara & Rob

March 31st

Room 402. I placed my reading glasses on the twelve-inch wide window ledge before I went to sleep. I had the window open about a half an inch. Sometime in the middle of the night, my glasses somehow fell off the ledge and landed on my pillow, waking me up. I doubt the wind was strong enough to blow my glasses off the ledge. I know I had set them way back on the shelf.

Wendy

April 8th

I was locking the door to my room when I felt and heard someone walk by me. I looked up to see who it was and to say *hi,* and no one was there.

Chris

April 9th

Room 315. My husband and I enjoyed our room very much. The first night of our stay we had no sightings. However, the second night while I slept, my husband felt a presence around him as they pulled and tugged on his gold chain. He awoke thinking it was me, but I was sound asleep.

Dennis & Linda

April 9th

Room 316. We felt the presence of the female ghost "Julia" from the moment we checked into our room. We also believe we saw her image by the window. We loved the room. This town is beautiful. We will be back. Everyone was great. A beautiful weekend getaway.

Lisa & Robert

April 14th

My wife left our room at about 10:20 p.m. and woke me up from a nap when she left. I thought I was alone, until I heard the rustle of paper behind me.

Paul

April 14th

No ghosts, but a piece of paper did mysteriously slide under the door to our room.

John & Mary

April 17th

Room 313, 2:30 a.m. I felt the bed shake once, lengthwise (not side to side). At first I thought it was my wife moving around on the bed, but she was fast asleep and lying on her stomach. Nothing else happened until I began to hear a buzzing sound in my ears and the buzzing increased in volume. At that time, the bed shook lengthwise again approximately six times in a rapid succession. I then thought it might be an earthquake! Then it felt as if someone was breathing on my bicep area. My wife was not turned toward me, so it was not her. I kept feeling intermittent shaking of the bed until the volume of buzzing in my ears receded.

Alfred

April 19th

Room 317. I was awakened by a noise, finally realizing it was coming from the bathroom. I went to look and see what it was. Opening the door. I was greeted with the image of a woman dressed in white.

No Name

April 22nd

Room 211. We left the small light on in the bathroom. We later found it turned off, and neither of us had been in the bathroom.

Joe & Cindy

April 26ᵗʰ

Bed remade twice in one day! No maid service.

Annie

April 30ᵗʰ

Room 301. I laid out a Baby Bop musical animal, hoping for the little boy to come. He didn't. But I awoke at 12:30 a.m. and found as normal, I was laying with my feet off of the end of the bed. I felt the strangest, light sensation, though not ticklish, brush against one foot (just the top) and mere seconds later the other foot.

Curt & Germa

May 6ᵗʰ

At about 3:45 a.m. I was awakened to the sound of my cup of water tipping over for no reason. I looked around but didn't see anything. In the morning the ring that had been on my finger was on the back of the nightstand.

Melanie

May 7ᵗʰ

Room 406. Upon arrival for our girls' weekend, skepticism sprouted among us. However, when we turned in for an early evening, we drew the blinds in anticipation of the early morning light. The blinds retracted suddenly and mysteriously with no provocation.

Teri, Jamie, Deb, Theresa

May 15th

Room 202. Sorry no sightings, just a lot of late party people making a lot of noise. We (my twin sister and I) celebrated our 49th birthday here. It was great.

Mary & Marion

May 15th

I got into the shower and had left my jewelry and a very large book on the nightstand. When I got out of the shower, my book and jewelry had been strewn about the floor.

Yvette

May 22nd

Room 315. I stayed in the "Julia" room two years ago. While attempts to dry my hair with the hair dryer did not work, I became frustrated. After I pulled the hair dryer off the wall, I immediately asked Julia to help me. No kidding, five seconds later the hair dryer worked.

No Name

May 30th

Thoroughly enjoyed my stay. Love Bisbee.

Andree

June 4^(th)

Room 406. Though we were on the top floor, we heard people above us walking around. We smelled the aroma of a cigar, very faint and only on one side of the room, that became stronger as the night got later. Sounds of kids running up and down the hallway between 1:00 a.m. and 2:00 a.m.

The Reisers

June 4^(th)

Room 401. My friend and I went to sleep around 10:00 p.m. I woke up very hot and kicked the covers off. I looked up and thought I saw my friend at the window. I thought she was turning on the air conditioner. The next morning I realized that the air conditioner was not on and that it was not in the window I saw my friend at. She said she had not been out of bed all night long.

Julie & Julie

June 6^(th)

Room 313. A little after midnight I was awakened twice by a sudden noise. The next morning I found my copy of the *Maltese Falcon* on the floor. When I had gone to bed, it was on the desk, far from the edge.

Rod

June 7^(th)

Room 406. While my friend was able to fall asleep, I was unable to. The air conditioner kept going on and off keeping me awake. Finally, I sat up in my bed, and in front of the mirror I saw a woman dressed in white, brushing her hair. She turned toward me, smiled, and then disappeared.

Guadalupe & Elizabeth

June 9th

We had the windows open in our room — still, no breeze. However, the door to our room opened and closed as if it was opened by the wind.

Meaghan

June 11th

Room 301. While watching TV late at night, we noticed the curtains move, just a small amount. Later in the night we noticed two white figures in the corner of the room in front of the mirror.

Sue

June 13th

Not able to sleep, around 3:00 a.m. I decided to walk around the building and head up to the 3rd floor balcony for a smoke. On the way up to the 3rd floor, I noticed a black figure in the stairwell. As I rubbed my eyes to focus, it disappeared. I continued up to the balcony and sat down. I looked to my left and noticed the same type of black figure. Again I rubbed my eyes. While I was doing this, I felt something touch my right arm. Startled, I opened my eyes and jumped up. The black figure was gone.

Allison

June 16th

Room 409. After unlocking the door to our room and turning on the light, I turned to pick up the luggage and enter the room. As soon as I entered, the lights started to flicker and then went out. I turned the light switch on and off a couple of times. The lights would come on and then flicker and go out. After about four times of doing this, the lights stayed on. Trying to sleep, most of the night I just tossed and turned. I could feel a presence in the room. At 3:30 a.m. I was awakened once more by the feeling of someone trying to push me out of the bed. The next day I decided to move rooms for the remainder of my stay.

No Name

June 29ᵗʰ

Room 308. All night long my little sister kept calling out in her sleep, "Who is that man over there?" and "Who are you?"

No Name

June 30ᵗʰ

Just after we went to sleep, we heard a noise. Sitting up, we noticed that a watch and a Hawaiian lei we had set on the dresser were now on the floor.

No Name

July 1ˢᵗ

Back on July 3, 2004, I stayed in Room 312. While I was laying on my bed reading, the door to our room opened. I thought it was my son coming into the room. I waited a few minutes and then went to the door and found no one there. This trip I came by myself, and once again while I was reading, the door opened -- and still no one there.

R.G.

July 3ʳᵈ

What a wonderful hotel. The staff was exceptional, and we loved our room. The entire stay was like a step back in time.

Sue & Paul

July 5th

Room 305. My husband was lying in bed in the morning alone in the room when he heard the bathroom door shut and the sink faucet turn on. He got up and knocked on the door asking for me, thinking I had come in. The door to the bathroom was previously left open because he had just been in there. Not receiving an answer when he knocked, he opened the bathroom door to find the lights and faucet off. He then went and laid down and once again heard the faucet turn on. I walked in the room at this time to find him completely confused and perplexed at what just happened. Regardless of what ghosts reside within the Copper Queen Hotel, we will always love it. We got married in the hotel last November.

The Teel-Foggs

July 6th

Room 406. About 3:00 a.m. the phone rang with a message from one of Room 409's guests, a little girl about six years old, saying she was worried and wanted her grandma to come to her. When we called the front desk to see what was going on, they informed us that there was no one in Room 409. However the last guest was three days ago, and indeed it was a grandmother and her granddaughter.

No Name

July 7th

My eight year old son Joel was talking to what must have been the little boy ghost as there was no one else in the room. He was trying to solicit a response and got very spooked when he heard giggling and footsteps running down the hallway of the 4th floor.

Michelle

July 24th

Room 409. Last night my son heard what sounded like cracking knuckles near his bed and saw a light orb pass through the room. Later on he heard what sounded like water dripping, as if the shower in our room had just been used. We all heard a scraping noise, like someone was dragging fingers across the screen to the window. (We were on the 4th floor.) My son ended up in our bed for the rest of the night. This all happened between midnight and 5:00 a.m. We decided not to stay a second night. My son wants to get some sleep, as do we.

The Rodriguez family

July 31st

Room 412. Last night we had an experience very similar to that which was recorded earlier in Room 409. At 12:32 a.m. the TV came on. We promptly turned it off, and then other strange things began to occur. We heard four distinct booming sounds from the hallway, like a large object was being dropped. We heard a trickle of water near the bathroom, along with a voice (low and deep) calling out names. Three times we heard a scratching noise above our heads, along with three flashes of light that filled the room. All activity ended by 4:30 a.m. A sleepless, yet interesting night in Bisbee.

The Three Travelers

August 7th

I woke up about 3:00 a.m. out of a deep sleep. I heard a woman humming. I woke my husband, and he said he never heard it. It was like a woman hums when she is dressing.

No Name

August 11th

Room 403. I moved the alarm clock so that my friend and I could both see it. In the morning we found it had been moved so that neither one of us could see it. We also noticed the candy that we had placed on the dresser was missing.

Joan & Martha

August 18ᵗʰ

My husband and I just stopped in Bisbee for dinner. We actually are staying in Tombstone. We came in for a drink in the saloon. When I walked in the saloon door, I had a major déjà vu experience. The sign over the door, the nude woman in the painting along with the red paint, it's all there. I have never been here before.

Lisa

August 23ʳᵈ

Room 410. My son (six years old) wandered into the bathroom, talking very softly to the point I could not understand what he was saying. When he came out, he said he had heard someone whispering his nickname, then his real name, and it was coming from the bathroom. We were the only two in the room.

L.M.

September 2ⁿᵈ

Room 308. When we first opened the door to our room, we smelled a very strong smell of cigar smoke. We called the front desk and asked for a room that was not a smoking room. They informed us that all of the rooms were non-smoking. Later in the evening as we were looking around the hotel, we smelled a strong perfume smell in the hallway that the Teddy Roosevelt Room is in.

Ashley & Cheryl

September 6ᵗʰ

Room 311. From the second we walked into our room, we could feel a presence in the room, as if we were being watched. My wife could not sleep; she kept waking up because she heard a woman talking.

A.A.L

September 18ᵗʰ

Last night I was waiting for the elevator on the 3rd floor, when out of the corner of my eye I saw someone walk behind me. When I turned to say *hi,* there was no one there.

Arline

September 28ᵗʰ

My husband and I stayed in the John Wayne Room last night. Waking in the morning, we found that the mirror above the dresser had what looked like two sets of lip prints on it, as if some one was kissing it.

Linda

October 8ᵗʰ

Room 308. During the middle of the night my sister was awakened by conversation right next to her. Thinking my niece was on her cell phone, she found that my niece was fast asleep. We found out later that my son had seen a shadow cross the room before he went to sleep.

Laura

October 13ᵗʰ

Room 409. We decided to stay here for our sisters' weekend away. We had a great dinner and the room was great. We had some experiences on the 2nd floor, with the smell of a man's cologne in one area with no one around. Then, in our room we were sure we had both room keys on the desk, and when we were going for breakfast, we only found one key on the desk. We looked all over the room for it, and finally found it under one of the beds. How in the world did it get there?

Gail, Donna & Margaret

October 20ᵗʰ

Right around Room 403 you could smell cigar smoke.

No Name

October 22ⁿᵈ

In the area leading to the pool area – the hallway that 207 is in – you could feel a very strong presence of people, but you don't see anyone. On the 3rd floor I felt the same type of presence on the west side of the building. Up there, you could feel it get stronger if you speak to it.

David

October 22nd

Great time once again. Thanks.

Phil & Ruby

October 30th

Room 204. I was wearing some skull earrings and had taken them off and placed them on the counter in the bathroom. In the morning there was only one earring on the counter. I found the other one underneath the sink overhang where it could not just have fallen.

Anita

November 8th

We immediately felt a presence in Room 204, along with a strange odor. We decided to ask for a room change and were moved to Room 304. The room was fine, but while I was drying my hair in the morning with my new hair dryer, it stopped. Suddenly, I felt the same type of presence I did in the other room. I decided to let my hair air-dry, but prior to checking out and packing my hair dryer, I decided to try it once again. It worked just fine, and no feeling of the presence.

No Name

November 18th

I could not sleep. I decided to go to the 2nd floor sitting area to read. Wow, you can truly feel them.

No Name

November 29th

Room 407. Heard whispering all night long.

No Name

December 6th

Room 406 is haunted.

No Name

December 18th

Room 315. I woke up feeling something very cold on my thigh. Then I heard talking but could not make out the words. My partner was sound asleep. The talking got louder and I could hear, "Go home, go home," and then felt a breath on my neck.

Greg

December 28th

Dear Future Guests, this hotel truly is haunted….
As I was in the shower with my lady, there was constant knocking on the bathroom door. We were the only two in the room. Good Luck

No Name

January 1, 2006

~

December 31, 2006

Copper Queen Hotel
Ghost Journal

January 2nd

We had left the window in the bathroom open when we left for the day. When we arrived back to our room, it was closed almost the whole way. When we later opened it again, it slowly closed again. After we awoke in the morning, the curtain fell to the ground.

The Brines

January 8th

Room 316. We were watching TV and then turned it off with the remote to go for dinner . When we arrived back to our room over two hours later, the TV would not turn on. We followed the electrical cord and found that someone had turned off the power switch. How?

Joan & Terry

January 13ᵗʰ

Thanks for the fun! We had a great time.

Randy & Deborah

January 14ᵗʰ

Room 317. I woke up at 12:30 a.m. to a very strong perfume smell. It was so strong that I opened a window and then fell back asleep. Was awakened again at 1:15 a.m. with drawers opening and closing in the dresser. I thought I was dreaming, but my friend woke up to the same events, also.

Jean

January 16ᵗʰ

Room 309. A lot of energy and activity in this room. Last night the bathroom door opened and closed a number of times. At one point the lights flickered on and off and the shower sounded like it turned on slightly. Then we noted that it dripped all night long. We continuously heard a woman's voice singing in the hallway, yet when we checked there was no one there.

Ashley

January 21ˢᵗ

Room 314. I had left my shoes in the bathroom when I went to bed. In the morning they had been moved from the bathroom to the other side of the room next to the bed.

No Name

January 24ᵗʰ

When I was in the dining hall, I looked to my left and for a split second I saw four gentlemen sitting at a table dressed in old time Victorian wear and seeming to be celebrating, one with very long bushy sideburns and another with a beard. When I turned to look again, they were gone. I checked with the hostess; she told me there had been no one sitting at that table.

No Name

January 26ᵗʰ

Room 208. When we woke up this morning, my husband's shoes were placed against the door of our bedroom leading to the outside hall. The shoes were propped up, placed in a position that we would have never done.

Bonnie & Rich

January 29ᵗʰ

Room 406. My husband and I travel frequently. This was one of the most comfortable nights we have had in a bed away from home. The ghosts – well, they must have liked us. Besides the occasional feeling of not being alone and only to turn and find no one there, we had no happenings.

Trey & Charlotte

January 29ᵗʰ

We always enjoy it here. We come once or twice a year on the motorcycles. See ya again.

Jim & Debbie

February 2ⁿᵈ

What a wonderful stay.

Thomas A. Waldorf, of the Waldorf Astoria & Waldorf Toiletries Company, and wife Melba. Also in party, the famous Roy Shaw & wife Molly from Bradford England.

February 3ʳᵈ

What a great stay, beautiful room, wonderful and kind people. We came looking for our family history. My grandmother worked at the

Copper Queen Hotel in 1916-1918, not sure. My grandfather worked in the mines. My aunt is buried in the Bisbee cemetery. She died Christmas day, 1916 at the age of eight days. We have learned so much.

Cindy

February 16th

I will be watching for you some night, as I sit in the unlit lobby.

No Name

February 16th

Room 217. We returned to our room after having a great dinner. We had picked up an after-dinner mint on our way out of the restaurant and had placed it on the corner of the dresser in our room for the morning. When we awoke in the morning, the mint had been moved to the middle of the dresser.

Mitch

February 17th

We had been drinking wine in our room. We corked the bottle and went out. When we got back to the room, the bottle of wine was uncorked and almost empty. The cork was in the trash can. Apparently, one of the ghosts is a fan of Merlot.

Jasmine & Ryan

February 21st

Room 407. I was lying in bed and kept waking up. One time, out of the corner of my eye, I saw a white light that appeared to the left of the bed and move across the room and then vanished.

John

March 8th

Room 406. We stayed in the Teddy Roosevelt Room and found Johns' eye glasses were moved during the night. We didn't hear a thing.

John & Fay

March 19th

As we were walking the halls of the hotel, we ended up on the 4th floor. As we were walking past the elevator, the doors suddenly opened. No one had pushed the *call* button, and no one was on it.

No Name

March 19th

Room 216. We left our video camera on all night long, and had left two drinks on the night stand next to the bed. This morning we found only one drink on the night stand, and my purse had been emptied out onto the desk. My book of angels that I have been reading was taken out of my suit case and placed on the stand. A number of lottery tickets were missing. The camcorder recorded a number of shadows through the room and recorded my mom talking in her sleep about some one holding her down and about getting the chains taken off her in her sleep.

Tracy

March 24th

Room 406. I was in a sound sleep, when at 2:00 a.m. I was awakened by someone or something breathing , very warm breaths on my right ear. I didn't see anything, but will definitely not forget the feeling.

John

March 24th

Remember where you put things, they may be moved.

No Name

April 11th

First time here. What a wonderful experience, a step into the past. Loved the antiques and architecture.

Stan & Jane

April 15th

Room 214. The right bedside table drawer opened by itself in the middle of the night. We noticed it around 1:30 a.m.

Meg and Bill

April 15th

I was walking down the hall to the restroom on the 1st floor when I heard a voice behind me. I turned around and saw a woman behind me. I said, "Sorry, I thought you said something to me." She said, "No, but I heard someone. too." There was no one else in the hall.

Jill

April 18th

Room 414. While we were playing a board game, the door to our room opened on its own. We had noticed the doorknob turn just prior to this happening. After the second time of this happening, we decided to leave and go down to the Saloon. My aunt needed to go back upstairs to get something and noticed the light we had left on was now off.

No Name

April 18th

Room 307. Early morning brought an unrolled roll of toilet paper onto the floor of the bathroom. Not just unrolled, but folded back and forth and still attached to the holder.

Debbie & Paul

April 21st

After getting into bed, I turned off the bedside light. I had left the light on in the bathroom to see, if I had to get up in the middle of the night. When I awoke this morning, the light was off.

Courtney

April 24th

Room 406. On the wall between the closet and TV, I saw a shadow on the wall. It appeared frequently through the night. It moved around, so I know it was not just a dark spot on the wallpaper. Also, around 3:00 a.m. I saw three lights that appeared on the exterior and adjoining room doors, then moved around the ceiling in all directions.

Sue

April 26th

My wife's hair brush was on the dresser. When we returned to the room, it was on top of the TV. I didn't tell her about the ghost in the hotel until we checked out of our room because she made us move out of our house back home in Lake Geneva because of ghosts, and I really didn't want to check out in the middle of the night.

John

May 7th

Room 401. Awoke at 12:30 a.m. and got up to turn off the bathroom light. I saw the "Do Not Disturb" sign on the inside of the door swinging back and forth slowly on the doorknob. There was no fan on nor any drafts through the door. The door was bolted shut.

No Name

May 7th

Room 406. Went to bed with the bathroom light off. Woke at 2:30 a.m. and found it was on.

No Name

May 7th

Room 409. The block of wood that held the window up suddenly fell off the ledge. It looked like it had been pulled out, and ended up about five feet from the wall. The window fell to the sill and shattered.

No Name

May 10th

Room 313. Kept being awakened by the smell of cigar smoke.

Art

May 25th

Room 308. I believe that Julia paid me a visit last night. I heard a woman's voice and then saw a white cloud in the corner of the room.

No Name

May 26th

Returning and entering into our room around midnight, it looked like someone else was in our bed, and wearing my nightgown. Screaming and going back to the hallway, we closed the door, thinking we had gone into the wrong room. We went down to the front desk, and they confirmed our room key as the room we were in. The clerk took us back up to the room and found no one, just my night gown on the chair. I had left it in my suitcase.

Ann

May 27th

Room 214. Nothing happened really, just noises in the middle of the night. But you know they are here; you can feel them.

Rachel

May 30th

We heard loud moaning as we exited the 2nd floor elevator. It sounded like a small child. We also heard what sounded like the chain of a swing in the air. Then the curtains blew open around the windows.

James

June 3rd

Room 312. I woke up at 3:15 a.m. to use the bathroom. When I returned to bed and relaxed, I began to feel a vibrating sensation through-out my body. I couldn't stop it. I had no control over it. After it passed, I felt frightened but tried to relax again. A short while later I began to hear a female voice singing. Then the vibrating, humming sensation began to pass through my body again. I was trying to cry out because I was frightened. After it stopped, I was too scared to sleep.

Rose

June 3ʳᵈ

    Room 311. I woke up three times throughout the night to the sound of a man whistling in the room.

Rachel

June 3ʳᵈ

    Room 315. We went to bed around 1:00 a.m. All night long my body was tingling as if someone was trying to hold me. My girlfriend woke up around 3:00 a.m. to see an indentation in the couch, followed by a stream of smoke.

Frank & Jaci

June 4ᵗʰ

    Room 314. Unable to sleep, at 3:00 a.m. I got up and was going to take a walk around the hotel. As I was leaving the room, I walked past the mirror over the desk and saw the form of a woman in it. I decided to stay out of the room the rest of the night.

Austen

June 7ᵗʰ

    Room 205. We left to go to dinner. When we arrived back to our room, there was the distinct smell of a different type of perfume, not my fiancée's.

David & Jackie

June 21st

Room 312. While the family was asleep, I was awakened by the sound of something rattling. It ended up to be the plastic on our water bottle case. I tried to doze back to sleep, then heard yet another sound. It was someone or something going through the suitcases. I thought my mom was up looking for something. When we all awoke in the morning, everyone said they had not been out of bed all night long.

Kyle

June 22nd

While I was watching TV, the volume continued to go up and down all on its own. I also noticed an old gum wrapper under the bed. I figured that housekeeping just missed it when they cleaned the room. In the morning it was gone.

Hunter

June 22nd

What a great summer getaway.

Mac & Anita

July 1st

Room 414. My daughter's cell phone was shut off. In the middle of the night it started to ring and ring. When she went to check the missed calls, there weren't any.

The Hartlands

July 10th

Room 401. All night long there was a tapping noise coming from the bathroom. In the morning all of the cupboards were open.

No Name

July 10th

Room 412. Upon arriving back to our room, we found one of the pictures on the wall turned sideways. This caused us a very sleepless night.

Chris & Jeannie

July 12th

I could not sleep and decided to take a bath at about 2:00 a.m. While I relaxed and soaked in the tub, I started to drift off to sleep. Suddenly, the light went out and I heard a woman's voice say, "Get out, come with me." Startled and thinking I was dreaming, I sat straight up and found that I had not been dreaming. The lights were out. As I moved the curtain aside, I saw a whiff of white smoke.

No Name

July 12th

Room 210. It appears that the ghost likes to move shoes. Mine were moved from one end of the room to the other end. My mom had a pair of socks tucked in the top of her shoes, and in the morning they were missing. Later she found them in her suitcase.

Miranda

July 12th

Thanks. Visiting with my daughter from California, in from

Tucson. We had a wonderful stay. The bed fell down but, oh well, it was fun. The staff and the owners were great. Thanks for a great stay.

Carol

July 16th
Room 207. The TV kept turning off, like there was a problem with the electricity in the room, but the lights were just fine. When we left for dinner, we left the TV on. When we returned, the TV was still on but on a different channel.

Gloria

July 16th
Room 210. We were in bed when we heard a crash in the bathroom. Upon entering, we found our shampoos were in the sink. We snapped two photos; the first one showed a shadowy smoke, and the other one showed an orb in the corner. Later that night we were awakened by children laughing and carrying on.

Dana

July 19th
Room 312. In the corner by the door, it had a very strong smell of cigar smoke. Also, at 12:00 a.m. I heard kids running down the hall. I opened the door and found no one in the hallway.

Kacy & Tess

July 29th
Room 202. About 7:30 I was going to take a shower and had placed the bar of soap in the soap holder in the shower. A few minutes

later as I was getting into the shower, the soap lifted up off the soap holder and fell to the floor, as if some one picked it up and then dropped it.

Fred

August 7th

Room 401. We checked into our room around noon, left our luggage and went out to walk the town. When we got back to our room, we found that our luggage had been unpacked and all of our clothes placed on the beds. Checking with the front desk, we were informed that housekeeping does not unpack luggage.

No Name

August 9th

Room 312. I had purchased a small bag of quartz rocks and had them by my bed when I went to bed. In the morning the bag was gone and could not be found any were in the room.

Erik

August 19th

Room 414. I was alone in the room and taking a shower. I heard a rattle at the bathroom door as if someone was trying to come into the bathroom. I went downstairs to my friends' room and asked if they were up in my room trying to scare me. They all said *no*!!! Who was it then?

Rick

August 23rd

Excellent service, most enjoyable stay!!! Will be back very soon.

No Name

September 4th

Room 303. This hotel is amazing. Our room was small but very cozy, just enough for the two of us. As for any sightings, we did not see anything. However, my boyfriend fell asleep first and I stayed up watching a movie. I fell asleep with the TV on. My boyfriend woke up to use the bathroom and turned off the TV. I could have sworn I heard a woman laughing. It's hard to explain because it was like lingering or coming from the air and only for a few seconds.

Kimberly & Bryan

September 18th

Room 217. First time here. Excellent hotel! My cell phone kept ringing my wake-up alarm even though it was turned off. My husband was awakened at 1:15 a.m. with a burning itching. We will definitely be back.

Helen & Rick

September 20th

Room 412. Great service and a very enjoyable stay. Your hotel is beautiful. Did not have the pleasure of meeting up with a ghost though. Would have liked that.

Julie

September 23rd

Terrific stay. Don't know who or what was playing with our doorknob while we tried to nap, but they sure were persistent. The knob was wiggled and turned at least three times over the course of about five minutes. We didn't hear any noise, footsteps or such before or after. Hmmmmm!!!

No Name

September 25th

Room 312. Early morning, I heard a tapping on the bathroom window. I was to afraid to look.

Helen

September 25th

Strong presence in bathroom of a child, while I was taking a bath.

Simone

September 27th

Room 308. I was reaching for the basket of lotions and shampoos and before I could touch it, it flew into the sink.

No Name

October 1st

Room 316. Broad daylight, bedroom drenched in sunshine. My husband's suitcase "fell" from the middle of the bed to the wall and floor under the window.

The Moores

October 4th

Room 305. It was great. Thank you.

Guy & Karen

October 5th

Room 305. My father was eating a burger that he brought to the hotel from Sierra Vista. After taking a couple of bites, he set the burger aside to finish later and he fell asleep. When he woke up, it was completely gone. At first I assumed he ate it, but the wrapper was not in the trash or anywhere in the room.

Lisa

October 12th

Room 211. My wife put her purse on the dresser before we went out for a walk in town. When we came back to the room, she asked me if I hid her purse. I had not. After several minutes she found it in the drawer below the TV. I did not put it there and she says she didn't either.

Jimmy

October 12th

Room 318. Very disappointed, no ghost activity in our room. Great night's sleep. We'll be back.

Jim & Karen

October 13th, (Friday the 13th)

Room 214. During the night we heard a door slam. It sounded like our bathroom door. We also heard the shower dripping water like someone just turned it off. When we checked, it was all dry. My jewelry was moved from one side of the dresser to the other.

Jackie

October 14th

Room 302. When we first arrived here at the hotel, my husband and I walked around the halls. As we turned the corner by the Julia Lowell Room, I snapped a picture of my husband by her door. All of a sudden I got a pain in my chest as if my heart was in pain; it stopped me in my tracks. We decided to go downstairs and rest in the lobby for a few minutes. This is when I read the history of Julia Lowell and how she had her heart broken and killed herself. Suddenly, I felt much sorrow for her and respected her for the tragic events in her life. My husband and I went back to our room to retire at about 10:00 p.m. It started off with restless sleep, and I awoke to my husband answering someone in his sleep, saying "Yes." I ignored this and continued with my restless sleep. I was then awakened to someone sitting on the right side of me near my feet on the bed. I was aware that someone was there, but I didn't feel threatened by this presence. I tried to doze back off to sleep when I felt them stand up off the bed, as if they went to do something and then later sat back down again. Suddenly, I felt a hand on my right ankle, a comforting hand, as if to say *it's ok.*

Rachel & Eric

October 21ˢᵗ

Room 404. Something or someone woke me with a shove around 2:00 a.m. You could feel the presence of someone in the room. I had a very strong feeling that I was suppose to go into the bathroom. After doing so, I looked out the window to end up looking at a wonderful meteor shower.

Tim

October 22ⁿᵈ

Both my husband and I had horrific nightmares all night long. I also heard doors opening and closing all night long, as well as strange voices in the hallway.

Angela

October 24ᵗʰ

Room 315. No Julia, but had a great stay. Looking forward to coming back.

Cody & Paula

October 25ᵗʰ

Room 317. We arrived in the early evening and detected a faint odor of floral pipe smoke. My wife thought it smelled floral, and I thought it was a bit on the smoky side, like a tobacco. I awoke at 3:56 a.m., uncharacteristically wide awake. I remained this way for nearly a full hour. The room felt comfortable and relaxing; however, at about 4:15 a.m, I noticed a thin veil of smoke entering the room through the outline of the door. My eyes were irritated, but I continued watching the haze fill the room, with unnatural slowness. After a few minutes of this, I decided to get up and check the hallway and see what was causing the smoke. Just as I was getting out of bed, there appeared the outline of a man dressed in a waistcoat, pacing back and forth in the smoke. Just as fast he was gone.

No Name

October 28ᵗʰ

Room 301. I was laying in bed with a pillow on my lap when I suddenly felt something try to pull the pillow away.

Audrey

October 29ᵗʰ

Room 409. About 5:30 a.m. as I was dozing in bed, I heard a knock on the wall, which is the outside wall to the front of the hotel. A few seconds after that, I felt as if my whole body was vibrating at an incredible rate. It lasted for about six seconds. I called out to my husband to tell him what was going on. As soon as he awoke, it all stopped.

Barbara

October 31ˢᵗ

Room 207. Scott, my husband, slept like a log. I, on the other hand, was awakened several times during the night by sounds at the door – the door handle being moved or touched, also scratching or the door by something like a piece of wood or a cane. Finally, fell asleep only to be awakened again by the smell of lantern gas, like the camping fuel you use for the old Coleman lanterns.

Mona & Scott

November 5ᵗʰ

Room 401. I woke to the bed shaking down by my feet. No one was there!

No Name

November 11ᵗʰ

Room 205. Entering my room at approximately 8:00 p.m., I hurriedly threw my suitcase on the bed as I needed very badly to use the bathroom. I noticed that my suitcase landed in the middle of the bed; however, when I came out of the bathroom, it was sitting nice and straight next to the TV.

George

November 17ᵗʰ

The door handle to our room giggled a number of times. Finally, I got up and opened the door, expecting to see someone there. No one was there, but I heard the sound of a child laughing and running down the hall.

No Name

November 19ᵗʰ

    Room 401. Staying alone this trip, I felt someone next to me, trying to cuddle in the night. I heard a woman whispering in my ear a number of times throughout the night.

No Name

November 19ᵗʰ

    Room 407. I had left my shoes in the corner of the room next to the adjourning door. In the morning when I woke up, they were in the bathroom.

Bill

November 19ᵗʰ

    Room 210. After a night of many strange noises, I decided to get up early and take a shower. When I was done and got out of the shower, in the steam on the mirror were the words, "Help me."

No Name

November 25ᵗʰ

    Room 301, 1:30 a.m. I heard a series of bells ringing and it woke me up. I thought it was my sister's cell phone, but when I asked her in the morning, there had been no calls.

Jeanine

November 26ᵗʰ

    Room 402. From about 2:00 a.m. to 6:00 a.m. there were taps and scratching on our window. We thought it was a tree, but in the morning we saw there was no tree by our window. Also, there were footsteps walking around our room this morning. You could definitely feel a presence.

Ashley

December 4ᵗʰ

Room 314. After a nice bath and preparing for bed, I brushed my teeth and went to bed. I was awakened twice in the night by what sounded like noises coming from the bathroom. In the morning my toothbrush was nowhere to be found.

Monica

December 6ᵗʰ

Room 312. At one point during the night, the desk lamp turned on all by itself. I was awakened at 3:30 a.m. by a noise in the room and thought I saw a shadow move across the room. Not able to sleep, I got up and looked out the window and noticed the form of a woman on top of the building across the street. In the morning I found out that building use to be the nursing quarters for the hospital.

Chris

December 6ᵗʰ

Had a great time here. Will be back again!

Sharon

December 21ˢᵗ

No active ghosts noticed. But while watching CNN and getting dressed for the day, I noticed the channels started changing all by themselves.

Manny

December 24th

Room 303. Lock your doors. All night long the door handles shake, and once the door opened. You can hear voices when you take a shower.

No Name

December 26th

Room 315. When we returned to our room after dinner, our bed covers had been pulled down, and things in the bathroom had been rearranged.

Betsy & Roger

December 27th

Room 403. Woke up at around 3:00 a.m. to a cigar smell. I was upset because I thought that maybe the room had been a smoking room. The aroma was rather pleasant, though. When we got up in the morning, the cigar smell was gone. I thought nothing of it until I saw the story at the checkout desk about the "smoking man." Oh, my gosh. We were visited by a ghost.

Mike & Robin

December 28th

Room 318. Walking up to our room, we smelled a very strong cigar smell in the hallway. Last night we took a lot of pictures in our room, and one showed an orb lighted up in the corner of the room. We also saw the pull cord on the desk lamp swing back and forth.

No Name

December 30th

Room 401. As soon as we walked into our room, the lights flickered as if someone was letting us know they were there. At about

12:00 a.m. I awoke to the TV still being on. As soon as I set foot out of bed, the TV turned off and the phone rang. When I answered it, no one was there.

Ramsey

January 1, 2007

~

December 31, 2007

Copper Queen Hotel
Now Open For 105 Years

January 4th

    Room 308. Make sure you have both lights on and the window closed in the bathroom, or you will hear a woman's voice, very faintly singing behind the mirror.

No Name

January 4th

    Room 315, when we checked in we did not notice anything

unusual. When we came back from a day of shopping and exploring the town we opened the door and were welcomed with a very strong smell of perfume.

No Name

January 6th

I can't remember when I have felt so welcome...although I did dream about cats all over my bed, but I loved them all. I will always remember my stay at the Copper Queen Hotel in Bisbee, AZ.

Pat

PS. You can't get there from here.

January 14th

Definitely ghosts!!! We were both in the bathroom this morning, sharing the sink when all of a sudden the ceiling exhaust fan came on all by itself. Oddly, I actually had to turn off the switch. (How had it been turned on?) We truly enjoyed our stay.

Peter & Ruth

January 21st

My girlfriend had what she thought was a nightmare in which an old man came out of our bathroom and scared her. She woke up yelling. She startled me and said she thought she saw someone or something in the corner by the door. She told me I had to stay awake and made me switch sides of the bed. So, needless to say, I was freaked out and wide awake for the next couple of hours. Every little noise put me on edge.

Mike

January 28ᵗʰ
    Room 317. Last night a few friends and I stayed here to celebrate our birthdays. Around 3:00 a.m. we were awakened by a loud clumping type of noise going down the stairs. Then all of a sudden we heard the sound of a little boy's laughter. We looked out the door and did not see anybody, but at the end of the hall-way in front of Room 312 there was a cloud of smoke. This morning there was a star cut our of paper on the floor outside our door.

No Name

February 3ʳᵈ
    Room 201. Between the hours of 1:30 a.m. and 2:00 a.m. there were repeated firm knocks on the door. When we called out and then checked the hallway, we found no one there.

David

February 3ʳᵈ
    Room 215. Fabulous stay. Celebrating our 27th anniversary.

Ed & Gretchen

February 4ᵗʰ
    Room 206. Our toiletry bag was on our sink all night long. In the

morning it mysteriously fell to the floor just as I was getting ready to take a shower.

No Name

February 9th

Room 311. At the verge of sleep, I heard a chain tap three times very loudly against the door to the room. As soon as this happened, I felt a cool breeze come across the bed.

Penny

February 11th

Sound asleep until 3:00 a.m. when I heard someone walking around our room. The footsteps started at the door to the room and continued all the way to the side of the bed that I was on.

Ralph

February 14th

When we checked into our room, the first thing my daughters said was, "Can you feel that?" Indeed, I could. You could feel a presence in the room. When we went to bed, we said a payer to keep us safe, only to be awakened at 3:00 a.m. to my son yelling and the sound of someone or something walking around the room.

No Name

February 15th

The thing we enjoyed the most was the gentle, transparent spirit.

No Name

February 18ᵗʰ

Room 409. At 6:30 a.m. I got up and turned off the light to the bathroom. As soon as I turned it off, I heard the door handle rattle and a kind of thumping noise outside the door to our room. I opened the door and found no one there. When we returned from breakfast, my daughter's purse had been moved from the desk to the bathroom counter.

No Name

February 21ˢᵗ

Room 201. I was awakened at 2:15 a.m. by the sound of someone in the room. It sounded like someone taking ice out of the ice bucket. I found my boyfriend sound asleep next to me, so I went back to sleep. In the morning we went to the 3rd floor balcony to have a smoke, and when we returned to our room, we found the change we had placed on the desk had now been moved to the nightstand by the bed. No one had been in the room at this time.

Shawna & Chris

February 21ˢᵗ

I stayed in this hotel about five years ago somewhere on the 4th floor. At that time I had some strange experiences. First off, when my friends and I were trying to fall asleep, I thought I felt someone sit down on my bed. Then around 1:15 a.m. we heard some kind of clicking in the hallway. We looked out the door and did not see anything, but when I turned around and looked in the mirror on the other side of the room, I saw a woman with long, dark hair.

No Name

February 21ˢᵗ

Room 407. Between the hours of 2:00 a.m. and 3:00 a.m. our

room became very cold; you could actually feel a breeze. This was accompanied by a very strong smell of perfume.

No Name

February 22nd

Room 310. Almost too peaceful of a night. The ghosts must have all been sleeping.

John & Audrey

February 28th

Room 307. Between the hours of 2:00 a.m. and 3:00 a.m. we smelled a strong scent of perfume. Later in the morning we heard what sounded like marbles dropping onto the floor.

No Name

March 6th

Room 315. We took pictures of the room, and when we played them back, we saw many orbs. Also, when I opened the door to go downstairs, my mother was in the bathroom and saw a flash of white light go past her left shoulder towards the door I had just opened.

Chauncey

March 7th

Room 208. My husband had been sitting, reading just prior to going to dinner. When he stood up, an old pair of reading glasses fell to the floor. They were not his; we had never seen them before. We set the glasses on the counter, placed the window block on the window sill, and went to dinner. When we returned, the glasses were gone, the window was closed, and the window block was gone.

Peter & Jeanie

March 19ᵗʰ

 Room 402. It was about 2:00 a.m. when I was awakened by footsteps in the hallway, along with a banging noise. When I checked the hall, no one was there.

Andrea

March 22ⁿᵈ

 I was out on the 3rd floor balcony, enjoying a cigarette, when all of a sudden I felt a hand on my left shoulder. When I turned, there was no one there.

Dodi

March 31ˢᵗ

 Room 406. The bathroom fan turned on and off all by itself a number of times through the night.

Luann

April 1ˢᵗ

 "Help Me" appeared in the bottom right hand corner of the bathroom mirror.

No Name

April 2ⁿᵈ

 While my husband was checking us in, I used the bathroom down from the Saloon. While I was pulling the door open, I could feel the door being pulled back again. When I finally got the door open, I found that there was no one else in the bathroom.

Sandra

April 3rd

Room 312. I awoke at 3:00 a.m. to the sound of someone jiggling the door knob to our room. When I checked the hallway, there was no one there.

Sarah

April 4th

We belong to a group called "The Paranormal Project" and have been to many old mining towns throughout the west. We loved Bisbee and especially the ambience of the Copper Queen Hotel. We filmed and photographed throughout the hotel, inside and out. We stayed first in Room 412 and had set out coins, jewelry and the keys to our room. We took "before and after" pictures. One of the keys we set out ended up missing; we couldn't find it the next day. We also got a great picture of an orb outside the window of 315. Thanks for a great stay. We loved the décor and ambience!

Gary & Chase

April 8th

Room 319. About 10:30 p.m. we heard a woman shrieking. It was an unnatural scream/screech sound, not human sounding. This was followed by running footsteps down the hallway. When we checked, no one was there.

Jo Ann & Phil

April 14th

Nothing really happened to me, but it was an awesome stay. Loved the stories.

Mike

April 25th

Room 413. We didn't see anything unusual. Oddly, my mom and I woke up at the exact same time, in the middle of the night. We both felt strangely sick to our stomachs and very thirsty. Within about fifteen minutes we both felt 100% better. Maybe it was an unnatural presence.

Amber & Valerie

April 29th

Room 412. I was awakened at midnight by something tapping me on the head. My son and nephews were sleeping soundly, so I know it was not them. Again that same night, I woke up and was surrounded by the smell of heavy perfume.

Sarah

May 9th

Room 318. We turned the light on in the bathroom, then partially closed the door so there would be some light if someone needed to use the bathroom during the night . When we got up this morning, the light was turned off and no one had been up all night long.

Sue & Greg

May 20ᵗʰ

Enjoyed our stay here at the hotel. Very nice. It puts you back in time. Hope to come back soon.

Albert & Diana

May 28ᵗʰ

Room 315. While I was lying in bed relaxing and watching TV, the door to the TV cabinet closed all by itself, with a very fast slam.

No Name

June 1ˢᵗ

Loved the stay here. The first day of our visit our room keys were "lost." I had been writing postcards and had moved everything off the desk, including the keys, and placed them on the bed. We turned the room upside down looking everywhere. After about twenty minutes of looking, we found them back on the desk under the postcards.

Melissa

June 4ᵗʰ

Room 308. We had a pleasurable stay. My sister woke up at 1:00 a.m. after hearing a scream. She also heard a little boy's voice coming from the bathroom, it sounded like laughter. We also had an experience with a missing key. We had laid it on the desk when we went to bed and could not find it in the morning. We finally got an extra one from the front desk and went out for the day. When we returned, the key was in plain sight right on the floor at the end of the bed.

No Name

June 6ᵗʰ

Room 312. Girls' weekend out. Four of us shared a room and

had a great time. Just about midnight all four of us heard a tapping on the window. We thought it was just the wind but found that it was not windy outside. At 3:00 a.m. I felt someone sit down on the side of my bed. When I sat up, I noticed that all of the other girls were asleep. In the morning most of our toiletries were out of the bathroom and on the floor in front of the TV.

Lela, Kayla, Jamie & Geini

PS. The left side of the room is very, very scary.

June 7ᵗʰ

If there were any ghostly visitors, we slept through their visit, in a nice comfy bed and a cozy room!

Pam & Phil

June 14ᵗʰ

Room 308. Our alarm clock went off at exactly midnight. We had not set it to go off and found that the switch was not even on. We had to unplug it to get it to stop. At the same time we heard a noise and someone talking in the adjourning room. We were expecting our son in this room, so we opened the door expecting to see him and found the room empty.

Mike & Lila

June 15ᵗʰ

Room 414. Sometime in the middle of the night I felt someone sit down on the edge of my bed. Suddenly, I felt a pressure against my side, as if someone was trying to push me out of the bed and onto the floor.

Tom

June 23rd

We left a dessert, bread pudding, on the table in our room when we went to bed. In the morning it had been moved, and some of it had been eaten.

Bill & Cheryl

June 25th

Just visited for the day. While walking around the building, all was fine until I made it to the 4th floor. As soon as I stepped off the stairs, I felt a strong pressure in my chest and found it hard to breathe. As soon as we went back down to the 3rd floor, the pressure went away.

Jillian

June 27th

Room 305. My wife and I were just passing through on our honeymoon and decided to stay here on a whim. We checked in around noon, went to our room, changed, packed a backpack, and went out to take a walk and to explore the town. When we returned to our room, I found a belt buckle I had bought in Tombstone on the floor just inside the door. When we left, the buckle was still in the bag and packed in our suitcase. Later that night my wife and I went to the 3rd floor balcony, and then returned to our room around midnight to take showers and turn in for the night. While I was preparing for my shower, I could hear a dripping noise coming from the shower. When I got into the shower, I noted that it had not been dripping; it was very dry. I took my shower without further incident. When I got out and reached for my towel hanging on the back of the door, I found it gone. I called to my wife; however, she had gone down to the saloon to get us a couple of drinks. I found my towel folded lengthways in thirds draped across the back of a chair on the other side of the room. When my wife returned, I asked her if she had moved the towel, and she had no idea of what I was talking.

Oliver & Ashley

July 1ˢᵗ

Room 201. My fiancée and I stayed overnight, and found that during the night the selector switch on the A/C unit kept changing positions, and she would have to change it back. Also, various items were relocated in the room. One time during the night, I was in the bathroom and heard a deep sigh, like some taking a deep breath all around me. I could also feel a presence both then and numerous other times through-out the night. Had a wonderful stay and plan on another visit soon.

The Fosters

July 3ʳᵈ

Room 318. It was later in the night when I decided to brush my teeth and prepare for bed. While in the bathroom, I heard a deep laugh, like somebody was laughing at a joke. It lasted about half a minute. I don't know what it was; it could have been the TV in the other room. But it sounded like the laugh seemed to overshadow the commercial that was on.

Mathew

July 4ᵗʰ

Room 204. My sister and I shared this room, and we both had different experiences. I was awakened by the sound of the hangers in the closet banging together, and my sister felt someone sit on the end of the bed by her feet. She said it felt like a little person. Later in the night I heard footsteps going from the door to the bed, and my sister heard weird noises at the foot of the bed at the same time.

No Name

July 5th

Room 215. At approximately 2:00 a.m., while returning to my bed from the bathroom, I felt a strange presence in the room and became short of breath. The most frightening thing was that a small mirror that had been hanging on the wall over the desk was now on the foot of the bed.

Manny

July 3rd

Room 503. What a great room, so nice and quiet. We had a wonderful time.

Betty

July 7th

Room 211. As I was talking with my husband about John Wayne staying in the hotel, a well screwed-in picture of him fell off the wall. I was the other side of the room, and my husband was sitting on the bed; neither of us were anywhere near the picture.

No Name

July 7th

Just got married at the Copper Queen Hotel. It was a wonderful experience for all. Thank you. I think we scared all the ghosts that stay here. We love it here and will be moving here soon.

Peter & Kathie

July 7th

Room 315. We took a number of photos in our room that showed several orbs and two light streaks. Mike was awakened by someone playing with his foot. He thought it was me but found me sound asleep.

Mike & Kathy

July 13th

OK, where do I begin? I woke up at 3:00 a.m. and didn't fall back to sleep until about 5:00 a.m. I consider myself to be a spiritual, as well as scientific and analytical, person. What I and my husband experienced, I truly believe it was true spirits. I saw, felt and heard things during this period of time that I was awake. It was a little unsettling when I first woke up, but I decided to embrace the experience and just let it happen. When we first checked in yesterday and went to put our things away, I went to the bathroom and asked the spirits to visit us. Before that, I said a prayer of protection. Never did I feel actually scared. I think the little boy spirit and the female spirit may have been actually in our room. I felt a pressure on the bed, as if someone was gently climbing onto the bed between my husband and me. It also felt like there was some slight pushing on the bed, back and forth. I saw what appeared to be little sparks, a little mist, or a shadow (enough energy to see it) go from the left side at the foot of the bed to above that point to across the room to the foot of the bed and rest on the end of the bed. This spirit was very playful and loving. I told the presence finally, saying that my husband and I loved him, he was safe and he could go home to the light. I held my cross on my necklace. It seemed to have left for the night. My husband woke up again at 4:00 a.m. and said, "I wish those people would stop tickling my feet." This is definitely a charming, enchanting hotel with positive energy. The room was comfy and the staff was wonderful.

Bobbie & John

July 14ᵗʰ

Room 308. We experienced a few things in our room and in the hall. At times it was very hard to take a deep breath, as if someone was sitting on my chest. Down the west hall on the 3rd floor we could smell perfume when no one was there. During the night my wife felt someone pushing on the bed near her feet, and I was tapped on the head. I also heard a tapping on the window.

Justin & Julie

July 14ᵗʰ

I experienced two things – writing on the mirror "HI," and my hair clip was missing for a couple of hours and then reappeared right in the area where I had put it originally.

Sherri

July 18ᵗʰ

Last night I woke up and saw the bathroom door opening up. Everybody else was sound asleep.

Hadley

July 22ⁿᵈ

We had a two night stay. Both nights at 12:30 a.m. and again at 3:30 a.m. the room filled with the smell of cigar smoke and perfume.

Phyllis

July 28th

    Room 215. Early in the morning we heard what sounded like a little child laughing in the bathroom. Both of us felt someone squeeze our feet.

Vanessa & Brandon

August 4th

    While walking the 3rd floor, we heard and felt someone walking behind us. When we turned to say *hi*, we found no one there.

No Name

August 12th

    Room 317. After today I am a firm believer in the afterlife. A number of incidents occurred that scared me very much. First, I was walking down the hall on the 3rd floor and I felt as though someone was breathing down my neck. It just kept blowing on me. I was all alone, so I have to wonder what it was. Secondly, I was walking across the hall to my mother's room. My son was the only one with me; he is three years old. All of a sudden I heard the pitter-patter of little feet pass along side of us. As it passed, we heard a slight giggle and then it was gone. Then at 3:00 a.m. I woke up because it was so hot. I looked toward the bathroom and at the edge of my bed. I saw a beautiful woman with brown hair looking at herself in the bathroom mirror. I quickly turned my head in shock, and when I looked again, she was gone. I am a firm believer after my stay here. You will be, too.

No Name

August 22nd

    Room 202. Went to sleep with the TV off and the bathroom light on with the bathroom pocket door half open. At 5:00 a.m. the TV came on, the bathroom door was open, and the light was off.

No Name

August 26ᵗʰ

Room 315. My husband and I stayed in Julia's room. We didn't sleep at all! When we first walked into the room, the light blew out. Throughout the night my husband heard laughing and running through the hallway. He saw a ball of light go through our room and out the door. He was sitting on the edge of the bed and felt someone tickle his neck. I heard our plastic bag move, like someone was looking through it. I also set my wedding rings out the night before and marked where they were on the desk. The next morning they had been moved and turned two inches away from their marked spot. I also felt a tug on the covers at the end of the bed that woke me up. It's quite an experience, but plan on not getting any sleep if you stay in Room 315.

No Name

September 3ʳᵈ

Room 209. We enjoyed our visit and being "visited." My daughter's stuffed animal was moved from its side to its back. My jewelry moved several times. Our hotel key was found under the jewelry. When we were charging our cell phones, we had them lined up by my husband. Later we noticed that they had all been moved forward. While my family packed our car, I was alone in the room filling out the comment card when I heard a child's voice to my left say, "Mommy, help." While I admit to being sensitive, this was a first for even me. We loved the hotel and staff and will be back for sure.

Lisa & Tom

September 8ᵗʰ

Room 315. My husband felt a very soft pinch to his backside. He quickly looked up and saw a heat spot on the ceiling (blue and gold). It only lasted about ten seconds. In the morning after he took his shower, in the steam on the mirror was the word "Good."

No Name

September 14th

While in the dining room, I had my napkin on top of the table, and it moved from my place across the table to my brother-in-law's seat. He grabbed it and shook it out and gave it back to me. This was witnessed by several other people. In our room we found dried leaves that had been sprinkled between the top sheet and the bottom sheet, after the room had been cleaned. The head of housekeeping had to clean it all up and had no ideas on how they got there.

Ann

September 22nd

Room 317. The electric clock at the bedside flashed off when we returned to our room. We reset it and went to bed. Early the next morning the clock was flashing again.

No Name

September 22nd

Room 315. My husband had his covers tugged off his feet twice during the night. He did not see anything but definitely felt a tugging on the covers.

Cat

September 22nd

Room 301. I had a guest sit on the end of my bed. For sure!

Karen

October 9th

My husband and I were watching our kids swimming in the pool. We had been keeping an eye on the windows of the rooms above us on the top floor. We noticed a white blurred shape; it was not a light. Then as we both stared at the whiteness, it began to fade away, as if it were stepping away from the window. We were both witness to this.

No Name

October 9th

Room 406. We were staying in the Teddy Roosevelt Room. We had gone on a walk around town. When we came back, we heard water running in the bathtub. When we checked, it was dry. We also noticed that a number of our things had been moved from where we had left them to other places.

Emily

October 19th

Room 312. This room is a very special place. In the later part of the night, we walked the halls in an attempt to ghost hunt. While walking down the back hall, we saw a shadowed figure. When we saw it, we called out, thinking it was a person. But after we called to it, it was gone. Later as we slept, we were awakened to a child's laugh. The sound was hollow, yet definitely in the room.

No Name

October 22nd

   Room 302. Woke up several times over the past two nights to the sound of whispering.

Shannon

October 29th

   Room 318. Woke up at 1:30 a.m. Don't know if it was a dream or not, but it felt real, as if someone got in bed behind me and put their hands on my hips.

Kevin

November 1st

   Room 306. When we arrived to our room, we found the door wide open and the strong scent of cigar smoke. Around 3:00 a.m. we noticed lights around the door and the sound of someone running up and down the hallway. The temperature in the room fluctuated from hot to cold all night long.

Tanya

November 11th

   Room 401. Our first night we put the chain lock on the door. In the morning we found that the chain was off and the two deadbolts were locked. We also smelled the strong aroma of cigar smoke.

No Name

November 12th

   Room 201. We had a great stay. Last night my sister's teddy bear was moved from one end of the room to the other. Also, a number of my things were moved to different areas of the room.

No Name

November 21ˢᵗ

Room 406. Last night I was awakened by the sound of our door lock turning. When I sat up in bed, I saw that the lock had been turned to the unlocked position. Then I noticed a dark shadow go across the room.

No Name

November 21ˢᵗ

Room 315. We requested this room after watching "Ghost Hunters" on the Sci-Fi channel. I fell asleep while my husband was watching the TV. He woke me up yelling, "Oh, my god." The armoire door closed by itself. I also felt a tap on my knee cap

Trish & Ben

November 24ᵗʰ

Miss Jane, who is very open and in tune with the supernatural experiences, felt unusual energy coming from the middle of the 2nd floor lobby. It made her heart beat faster, and she felt motion sickness, almost to the point of falling over. I think if you stand in the middle of the 2nd floor lobby you will feel something, also.

Melanie

November 30th

Walked around the corner of the 2nd floor toward the pool and ran into a woman. I jumped back and went to say *excuse me*, but when I turned around, there was no one there. She was a brunette, about five feet tall, wearing a light brown/tan outfit.

Dennis

December 7th

Room 315. Well, it started out mild enough. My girlfriend and I came to this hotel to stay in the infamous Julia Lowell Room. It was pretty uneventful during the day, so we enjoyed Bisbee's antique stores and tours. When we finally came back to our room for the night, we took showers, put on the robes, and decided to take pictures. What we found when we reviewed them were small, round clouds of light – one above the painting of the woman on the wall, another above my girlfriend's head while she laid in bed, and three spheres which looked like they were floating up to the ceiling. During the night my girlfriend continuously woke up feeling another presence at the foot of the bed.

Alberto

December 25th

Christmas day in the dining room, my husband ordered a bottle of beer before dinner. The waiter brought it and poured it into a glass. We got up to go to the buffet table, and when we returned to the table, the glass was only half full.

J.B.

January 1, 2008
To
December 31, 2008

Copper Queen Hotel
Now Open For 106 Years

January 13ᵗʰ
      Room 402. My mother felt someone sit down on the foot of her bed.

                                                    No Name

January 19ᵗʰ
      Room 315. My husband and I checked in late afternoon. We were in the room for about one and a half hours, waiting for our dinner reservation downstairs. I took photos from different angles and especially of the area where the bed is, and when playing back the photos on our

digital camera, we noticed a white, fuzzy object at the foot of the bed. This image did not show up on any of the other photos. The white, fuzzy, round object was about the size of a baseball. It wasn't a reflection of anything around the room. We brought it to the folks at the front desk. They said it was an energy orb. Other guests have captured energy orbs and clusters of them in other rooms and hallways.

The Holmans

January 22nd

Room 313. My husband and I heard a boy running in the hallway and giggling very loudly at about 2:00 a.m. When we checked the hall, there was no one there. What a weird feeling.

Mike & Livea

January 22nd

Room 315. I woke to a booming voice, as though it was spoken through a fan. The room was freezing, and I had chills all over my skin. The temperature in the room read 72, but it felt much colder than that. I laid back down, and felt as though I was sinking into my bed with pressure felt on me and around me. I sat up and the pressure was gone. When I woke up this time, it was after 3:00 a.m., and the room felt much warmer again.

No Name

January 27th

Room 503. Something definitely moved my sunglasses across the room. In the middle of the night we heard voices in the room, but no one was there.

Jeff

February 2ⁿᵈ

Room 204. No ghostly encounters. Awake half the night to greet, but no one came.

Mike

February 4ᵗʰ

Room 216. Heard footsteps up and down the hallway all night long. Also, heard footsteps in my room and around my bed.

Doug

February 8ᵗʰ

Room 311. As soon as we entered our room, we heard a banging noise in the wall. This occurred three different times through the night.

No Name

February 10ᵗʰ

I had just finished the Old Bisbee Ghost Tour when I came in this beautiful hotel to view the ghost record. I glanced over at one of the mirrors in the back lobby and saw an older lady. She had long, wavy blond hair and was wearing a very short, red dress and was leaning against a wall. I glanced around the lobby, expecting to see her, but no one was there. This had me scared. I then glanced at the candle behind the desk when I saw a little red spark fluttering around.

Madeline

February 17ᵗʰ

Room 304. At 12:30 a.m. I was awakened by a woman sobbing outside the door. I looked out, and there was no one there. The ghost of Julia? Or a guest? We will never know. Maybe it was Billy's mom.

L.K.

February 24ᵗʰ

Room 318. Well, we were really not expecting anything to happen. Our room seemed fine all day, so we went about our day worry free. After a long day of walking the hills and enjoying a small town like this, we fell asleep. Somehow during our nap, the clock was unplugged and turned toward the wall.

No Name

February 25ᵗʰ

Room 301. My mom and I were staying here last night. Although not much happened during the night (except some strange dreams), this morning something strange happened. We had a fabulous breakfast and then returned to our room. I opened the curtains, and "LA" was written in lipstick on the window. My mom had left her lipstick in the bathroom, and now it was on the desk by the window. I have no idea what LA means.

Annette & Alison

March 6ᵗʰ

Room 407. I heard a woman screaming with much pain. It woke me up at 3:00 a.m.

Gloria

March 14ᵗʰ

Room 411. We heard the floor boards creaking in the middle of the night in our room. We were the only ones in the room.

Dave & Elaine

March 18ᵗʰ

Room 317. At 2:30 a.m. I awoke and felt as though I was covered in ice. I was freezing. Then I felt a cold arm lay across mine and clasp my hand. It was soft, like a woman's arm and hand. Then it was over, as fast as it started.

Jennifer

March 19th

Room 309. First we smelled an overpowering smell of jasmine perfume several times throughout the night. My boyfriend and I fell asleep. I kept waking up to whispering in my ear, saying "Shhhh." Then someone kept touching my right arm. I couldn't sleep. Then I looked over to the right side of the bed and saw a transparent woman glide past my bed and disappear. In the morning I found my undergarments twisted and all over the desk.

Jen & Jason

March 25th

Room 302. On and off we smelled the aroma of cigar smoke. Our ceiling fan was running, and we did not turn it on.

Dave & Linda

March 27th

High school sweethearts met again for first time in thirty years. We had a great time.

Pete & Lisa

March 29th

Room 401. At approximately 10:00 p.m. we smelled smoke and matches, along with seeing a light shadow that shifted colors. The smoke and match smell continued throughout the night. Also, if you take a shower, look for the initials "WH" in lower left hand corner of the mirror.

Chris & Laura

April 3rd

My husband and I were sleeping in one queen bed, and the blanket on the other bed was folded back. He was sleeping and I was watching TV when the blanket unfolded and fell down.

Julie

April 3rd

Room 407. This room has a large bed with three pillows. We thought it was a little strange but we went to bed anyway, the two of us on one side of the bed. At about 3:00 or 4:00 a.m. I awoke to find a body in the bed with us, his face inches from mine. Frozen with fear, I could barely breathe. I shut my eyes again, and when I reopened them, all that was left were a few hairs on the third pillow.

No Name

April 10th

When I found out that we were going to stay at this wonderful "haunted" hotel, the Copper Queen, I was so excited!! I couldn't wait to have a ghostly encounter, but alas – none. I thought for sure "Little Billy" would love to take a gander at all my "bling," but I guess he was busy getting into some other mischief. Our stay was wonderful. We hope to be back another time, then maybe see some ghosts.

Justine & Alan

April 12th

We had a nice stay, until some ghost decided they were colder than we were and pulled the covers off the bed; they ended up about three feet from the bed.

No Name

April 18th

Room 412. My earrings fell from the nightstand to the floor in the middle of the night. Loud, dragging noises on west side of room.

No Name

May 2nd

Room 315. My wife's chain was placed on the dresser nice and straight. In the morning it was curled like a snake. All of our coins were placed in a stack on the desk, and in the morning one of the quarters was found on the floor by the bed.

Ted & Susan

May 3rd

My husband and daughter left our room, and I got into the shower. While in the shower, I heard the bathroom door shake. When my husband and daughter returned, I said, "Very funny, shaking the door." They swore they hadn't returned to scare me.

Roxana

May 4th

Our stay was so nostalgic. It reminded me of Grandma's.

No Name

May 12ᵗʰ

My husband and I are believers but skeptics at the same time. Our first night we stayed in Room 316. We heard a noise in the corner that awakened both of us. We could not figure out what it was. In the morning we noticed something sticking out from under the dresser; it was a book of matches we had placed on the desk after lighting a candle. There was no way it could have fallen on its own. The second night we stayed in Room 315. My husband fell fast asleep around 11:00 p.m. I stayed awake watching TV, when right outside our door I heard lots of commotion and running up and down the stairs. I figured it was just other guests, but then my nostrils filled with the strong scent of a cigar. I waited a brief few seconds, and the noise in the hallway stopped and the cigar smell went away. About thirty minutes later, I heard what sounded like someone walking in our room and then the bathroom. I decided to get up and check out what I had just heard and found all of the drawers open; they had been closed just an hour earlier.

Doug & Shawn

May 16ᵗʰ

Room 401. My family and I went down to the hotel restaurant for dinner. When we left the room, my stepdad made sure to lock the door. We all saw him lock it. When we came back to our room after dinner, we found our door wide open. Nothing was missing, but how strange that the door we saw get locked was wide open.

Natasha

May 17ᵗʰ

My friend Janie and I decided to walk through the Copper Queen Hotel just for fun. While walking on the 3rd floor west side of the building, I smelled a strong but pleasant floral scent. Janie didn't smell it at first, but then also smelled the strong fragrance. As quickly as it came upon us, it disappeared. Very interesting!

Danielle

May 18th

Room 312. Last night as we went to bed, we placed a silver chain on the desk in our room. I awoke at 2:00 a.m. and noticed the chain had been moved a couple of inches. In the morning when we awoke, the chain was on the floor in front of the door to the room.

Jesse

May 18th

Room 412. When we left the room, we left the lights and the TV on. We went on the Old Bisbee Ghost Tour, and when we all came into the hotel, we opened our room for everyone to see. When we opened the door, we were shocked to find the TV and the lights had been turned off. This was a really fun place, and we had a wonderful time.

Angela

May 20th

I was terribly disappointed not to have had a ghostly experience, but that was my only disappointment. Wonderful hotel, fascinating town. I really hope I can return one day. Thanks for everything.

Gordon Watson

May 26th

Room 308. I heard footsteps from one end of the room to the other. Every time I would look up, I would find that no one was there.

Cyd

May 27ᵗʰ

Room 204. Woke up at 3:15 a.m. with all the hair on my body standing on end. I felt a strong presence of a person in the room, yet I didn't see anything.

John

May 30ᵗʰ

Room 412. I woke up and saw a shadow move near the far right window. Shortly after that, I heard heavy footsteps or like a stomping sound about seven or eight times.

Eileen

May 31ˢᵗ

Room 315. We stayed in Room 315 because it was on "Ghost Hunters," and we wanted to see the ghost. My cousin fell asleep around 11:00 p.m. I shut the TV off and shortly after could hear footsteps and shuffling at the foot of the bed. I fell asleep, and she awoke at 1:30 a.m. and heard the same thing!!!

Lynn & Gabby

June 7ᵗʰ

Room 403. I woke up at 2:30 a.m. to a very warm room even though the

AC was set at 70! Then woke up at 5:00 a.m. to find the AC turned off. Could it be the spirits were too cold?

No Name

June 10ᵗʰ

As we lay in bed trying to fall asleep, suddenly there was a crash in the bathroom. My husband got up to check and found his shaving kit on the floor of the bathroom. He said it was on the toilet tank and there was no way it could have fallen off all on its own.

No Name

June 10ᵗʰ

Room 412. There were five of us sleeping in the room; all but two of us were asleep. At about 11:00 p.m. the window sounded like it was being tapped with a metal latch about every forty minutes. Sometimes this would happen louder and faster than other times. This morning I checked to find there was nothing on the window to make the noise. Also, at 1:30 a.m. we heard laughing.

Sam

June 18ᵗʰ

Room 307. I am from Tucson. Somewhere around 1:00 a.m. in the morning, I felt the presence of another person in my room.

D.D.

June 22ⁿᵈ

Room 402. There was a knock that occurred twice on the door to our room. When I checked the hallway, I looked both ways and found no one there.

Stephen

July 4ᵗʰ

Room 315. My wife and I stayed in the Julia Lowell Room. This morning four drops of blood were found on the bathroom floor. My wife and I, both 69 years old, had stepped on the blood before we noticed it. Neither my wife nor I had any cuts.

Jim

July 7ᵗʰ

Room 213. My mother was in the bathroom and could not get the door open; it seemed to be stuck. Suddenly, the door opened all on its own. In the morning the door fell off its hinges, and we noticed a large print of a hand on the one side of the door.

Jessica

July 18ᵗʰ

My personal clock was on the bedside table when we went to bed. In the morning I found it under the bed up against the far wall.

Mary

July 21ˢᵗ

Finished at the bar at about 10:30-ish and headed up to my room by taking the elevator to the 3rd floor. I got out and started walking the short distance to my room when there was a sudden coldness to my right side, almost like a really cold draft. The hair on the back of my head stood up. There was nothing there. I got to bed rather quickly.

Johnny

July 25th

Sorry, but no ghosts!!! Excited though to stay in this fine old hotel. Thank you for the wonderful stay. Good Job!!!

Rich & Edward

July 27th

Room 401. When first arriving, my daughter and I felt a very strong vibration in the lobby. I felt like the elevator was going to close in on me. When I entered our room, I felt a pressure in my chest and in the middle of my forehead. I was very still and quiet for a long time. My boyfriend said he got chills when he was in the shower. My son kept saying that someone was playing with his hair. My daughter said she kept feeling a tickling on her shoulder and feet.

Catherine

July 28th

Room 210. Upon checking in, I unpacked my son's and my clothes and placed them in the dresser. In the morning my son noticed that the drawer pull on the dresser was gone. When I put our clothes in the drawer, I would have noticed the pull having been missing. I talked to the head of housekeeping and told her it was missing, and she informed me that it had been there the day before when they cleaned the room.

George & Chris

August 1st

At 3:30 a.m. I was awakened out of a deep sleep by a feeling in the room. I attempted to fall back asleep when I was disrupted by the same feeling and the sound of a little boy crying. We were the only people on this side of the building.

Christina

August 1st

After finishing the ghost tour, I looked up at the 3rd floor next to the balcony. I saw a tall man in a long, black coat look out the window and then lean back in. Then he was gone.

Paul

August 3rd

Room 401. My son awoke at 1:30 a.m., feeling as if someone next to the bed was staring down at him. He pretended to sleep, but the feeling was too strong. He jumped over his little sister, went to my bed, woke me, and said he was scared. Later I felt a couple of nudges against my bed (twice). I looked and saw that the kids and my husband were sound asleep. My daughter said she woke up and saw a figure of a man looking down at her parents asleep in bed. Definitely haunted here.

The T's

August 3rd

Room 412. While watching TV, I felt a presence in the room. I looked over my shoulder and saw what looked like the shadow of a little boy walking behind me. This gave me the chills. In the morning the change I had placed on the desk was missing. Later we found it under the bed.

No Name

August 8th

Room 212. About 2:40 a.m. there was the sound of children playing outside in the hall. A voice called out to someone named Billy. When I checked to see if I could help, there was no one there.

A. C.

August 14th

Room 205. The TV changed channels all by itself. After breakfast we came back and found that several items in the bathroom and in the room had been moved.

Michele

August 22nd

Took pictures on two different cameras, and all of them came out black, even with the flash going off.

Christian

September 5th

Room 315. I was awakened a few times during the night by tickling on the neck and shoulders, as well as whispering. My wife was next to me in bed, but the touch and sound were coming from the other side of the bed. Had a great stay here in Bisbee. We'll be back.

Jake

September 29th

Room 315. Took pictures in the room and found nothing odd or strange to report. We attempted to talk to Julia with no response, but the room started developing cold spots during the conversation. We took a few more pictures and caught orbs in places that previously had nothing.

No Name

October 10th

Room 401. We did the ghost hunt with Renée. When we did the Copper Queen Hotel part, we found the room with the most activity was our room. We spoke to Julia, asked her questions, and the K2 meter would go over. Strong perfume odor in the room. We also smelled a strong odor of cigars in the hallway on the 4th floor.

Bruce

October 16th

Room 318. Around 8:00 p.m. I was in the shower and heard over and over, "My name is Lilly." About an hour later I opened the hotel book in the room and found the page that tells about Lilly Langtry. Also, saw a shadow during the night, along with some pounding on the walls and a strong, cold breeze.

No Name

October 17th

    We spent last night in the Julia Lowell Room. When we got into the room, my husband went to set up his handheld tape recorder. When he hit *play*, the cover for the tape flew off, the tape came out, and the battery died. The thing is that it worked fine the night before at home.

                         LY. & Kevin

October 19th

    At approximately 11:00 p.m. my wife Dianna and I were just about to fall asleep, when I heard the sound of a small boy laughing outside our room's door. The next day I asked the hotel staff at the main desk if there were any families checked in with small children. They said no and told me who I heard laughing was Billy. On our second night at about 1:00 a.m., both my wife and I heard the sound of our spare change, that we left on the table, move back and forth.

                       Kent and Dianna

October 25th

    Last night I had actually forgotten about the "ghosts, " I suppose because I had so enjoyed the sights and sounds of Bisbee earlier that day, and wasn't focusing on them. That morning I had also told myself I would not be disappointed if I didn't experience anything unusual. Well, something did happen. Last night at 9:42 p.m. I smelled stale cigar smoke. It came and left three times. I could not smell it if I turned my head even slightly in either direction.

                             Lynn

November 2nd

    My husband and I stayed in Room 413. We went to bed around 1:00 a.m. I was a little scared and slept as close to my husband as possible. At approximately 3:00 a.m. I awoke to feel the sheets being pulled from me around my shoulders. I immediately grabbed my husband and whispered to him what had just happened. He didn't believe me. I laid in bed until I fell asleep hours later. Then around 5:00 a.m. my husband woke me and said that he felt something grab his big toe and tug on the blankets a few times. We will be back.

Matt & Tristan

November 9th

Room 402. In the middle of the night I woke up from a dream and lay awake trying to get back to sleep. I felt a hand on my right leg just above my knee. I could tell this was not a twitch, and it was not just pressure because I could feel each finger separately.

Melissa

November 10th

Room 419. I was sleeping when I was awakened by a tapping on the window. It became louder and harder until I responded to it. After I sat up, it stopped. This repeated four times through the night.

Bill

November 11th

Room 315. I experienced a feeling of being tickled and smelled a perfume. Other than that, nothing else happened in the room. But while roaming the halls, I smelled a cigar and heard kids running and laughing.

Stephen

November 15th

Room 414. Around 5:00 a.m. my cousin and I both heard the voice of a child babbling away. It seemed to be coming from the next room but was so very clear. We also noticed there were no adult voices. I asked at the desk this morning if a child was next door. The front desk informed me that the rooms on either side of us were vacant last night.

No Name

November 30th

Room 412. I felt a number of cold spots in different places throughout the room. I had placed a dime on the table, and it moved from one side to the other.

Shannon

December 10th

Room 315. First thing was that the battery for my camcorder was drained within an hour of being in the room. Then around 2:00 a.m. I felt my feet get uncovered. The sheet and blanket were tucked in, and I was not moving around. So I stayed awake for a while in the dark, and around 4:00 a.m. I felt something being pulled over the bed and then hitting the floor by the nightstand.

Kent

December 25th

Room 315. The temperature dropped drastically at the foot of the bed. I felt someone lift up the end of the bed and then drop it again at 1:00 a.m. We were once again awakened at 1:30 a.m. to the sound of footsteps coming from the bathroom to the foot of the bed.

Robin

Epilogue

The collection of eyewitness accounts you have just finished reading were from guests and staff of the Copper Queen Hotel, and were taken from the Ghost Journals which are kept on display at the front desk of the hotel. They are exciting, suspenseful and intriguing because they are the actual experiences of the guests themselves. Some of the guests were avid fans of the supernatural, and some were reluctant spectators who were caught up in their own experiences.

But this book would not be complete if we did not include the true-life incidents witnessed by Renée, the hostess of the nightly Old Bisbee Ghost Tour which always includes a visit to the Copper Queen. Over the years she has seen, felt and heard many things in the hotel. The following is a brief collection of some of those moments.

CQ

It was the night before Halloween, 2008, and Renée had two girls with her on the ghost hunt. They had just left Billy's Room and were walking to the fourth floor to visit Room 409, when they heard what sounded like male footsteps (from the heaviness on the treads) coming from the area near the elevator and moving in their direction. Renée called out, asking whoever it was that was approaching not to jump at them from around the corner and frighten the group. Her thought was that a local resident of Bisbee was attempting to sneak up on them and make them scream. The trio then heard a loud sigh. At that moment, one of the two girls on the hunt rounded the corner to see who it was, only to find the hallway empty. None of them heard the sound of departing footsteps.

CQ

One night during a ghost hunt, Renée had a mother and daughter with her in Billy's Room. The daughter had brought along her video camera. After leaving Billy's Room and moving to the fourth floor, the daughter noticed that the camera battery was inexplicably drained. According to

Renée, this is a common occurrence when there is paranormal activity. The daughter asked if she had time to return to her room for the spare battery. Renée told her that would be fine. The group listened to the daughter walk down the hallway ... open the door to her room ... and suddenly scream! Renée immediately ran to the room, only to find the daughter standing in the center of the hallway outside her door and pointing at the interior of the room. Looking in, Renée saw that there were marbles scattered all over the floor. Renée, of course, asked her if she had left them in that fashion, and the daughter explained that she had not and told Renée that, before leaving, she had placed the marbles in two rows between the two beds. She went on to tell Renée that she had also left a tidy stack of coins on the corner of the desk. The daughter then pointed out that not only had the marbles been scattered around the carpeted floor, the top four coins of the stack had been placed on the surface of the desk around the remainder of the stack.

CQ

A final story ... while Renée was conducting a hunt through Room 401, one of the members of the group, a teenaged girl, asked Billy to turn her flashlight on and then to turn it off. As she requested, her flashlight came on and then turned off. Renée was utilizing her EMF (Electro-Magnetic Frequency) readers at the time and, during this experience, the readings were quite high.